The Daily Telegraph

Cryptic Crossword Book
52

The Daily Telegraph
Cryptic Crossword Book
52

Pan Books
in association with *The Daily Telegraph*

First published in 2004 by Pan Books
This edition first published 2018 by Pan Books
an imprint of Pan Macmillan, a division of Macmillan Publishers Limited
Pan Macmillan, 20 New Wharf Road, London N1 9RR
Basingstoke and Oxford
Associated companies throughout the world
www.panmacmillan.com

In association with *The Daily Telegraph*

ISBN 978-1-5098-9387-4

A CIP catalogue record for this book is available from the
British Library.

Visit **www.panmacmillan.com** to read more about all our books and
to buy them. You will also find features, author interviews and
news of any author events, and you can sign up for e-newsletters
so that you're always first to hear about our new releases.

ACROSS

1 Unable to leave home – or travelling there? (10)
6 Medal struck before dinner (4)
9 Viewers should hold on to catch *The Poets* (10)
10 Unable to hear the fade out (4)
13 Is invited to define what the caller did (7)
15 Wine available to Arabs wandering about (6)
16 Made baby's bed in Berkshire (6)
17 It is in print, for crying out loud! (11,4)
18 Pretty useless hanger-on? (6)
20 Spanish place where drunken Nora hid silver (6)
21 Cast down drain (7)
22 A fish month in the Jewish calendar (4)
25 Drawback admitted by rebel leader to humorous poet (6,4)
26 Come down to earth (4)
27 Church member taking professional exam sitting by a social worker (10)

DOWN

1 Henry has stirred the re-heated dish (4)
2 The bone used in some beautiful Namibian carvings (4)
3 I need another hundred to make it like paradise (6)
4 Humble subscription by a deferential menial (8,7)
5 Being annoyed, informed the police (6)
7 Rook accomplished attack (10)
8 Present to little Ken on Sunday (4,6)
11 Target-round that is any colour? (6,4)
12 Parade for the said period (10)
13 Left act with Dave performing (7)
14 Meals eaten by those who eat meals around the north (7)
19 An article to be followed (6)

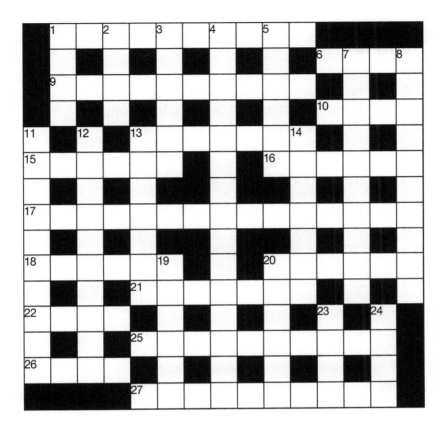

20 Remarks that are made incidentally (6)
23 Fellow recurrently dined on Greek cheese (4)
24 Does this work cause worry? (4)

ACROSS

7 Quarrelling pets (3,3,3)
8 Number at Welsh resort (5)
10 Don Brook creation that is turned by hand (8)
11 Sailor Bill uses half of the old counter (6)
12 Legendary works each containing identical Roman figures (4)
13 Spread all round city an area... (8)
16 Drink cocktail, looking wooden (4)
18 The intellectual had for example double trouble (7)
20 Account of refined 17 at Yarmouth school (7)
22 Little woman left an alcoholic radical (4)
24 Note with regret not all are revolting (8)
26 Pop group making a come-back unchanged (4)
29 Island paradise wherein a number take a German title (6)
30 Thrash, thrash, thrash (8)
31 Way to acquire wood store (5)
32 Wendy Sade went berserk in the middle of the week (9)

DOWN

1 Henry's on to a case which causes devastation (5)
2 It's senseless to dispose of foreign capital (6)
3 Paradise so long as beasts don't get toothache (8)
4 Grave nothing! The French take a chance with it (7)
5 Recollected having been summoned again (8)
6 How long does a boxing match last? Too long! (5,4)
9 Non-clerical member of US city is in charge (4)
14 Appeal to Catherine for approval (4)
15 Make situation worse for a Girl Guide initially, Virginia, in class (9)
17 Dame fell over cheese (4)
19 Eel sheds constructed despite the dangers (8)

21 One who petitions for wild animal caught outside (8)
23 Cereal food that is eaten by errant males (7)
25 Admits possessing (4)
27 A follower could get cook? (6)
28 Sounds metal, Rob! (5)

ACROSS

1 Looked sharp and got $1000 cut (7)
5 Clean son followed by a tiny young dog (5,2)
9 Boring thing to train recruits? (8,7)
10 Afternoon inspection (4)
11 Let it be put in place of a name (5)
12 Case for the sewers in the Tuileries (4)
15 Backdrop to the situation at railway termini (7)
16 Put up with Thomas C Strange (7)
17 Finished up in the brine rather drunk (7)
19 Not quite all there? That's rather unfair (1,3,3)
21 Unusual army troops (4)
22 Hal accidentally caught by a European mounted lancer (5)
23 Mount a little quiet nag (4)
26 Who, in the dog days, can become bitter-sweet? (5,10)
27 Looks after the geese? (7)
28 Casual wear for a Devonshire diner (7)

DOWN

1 Zilpah's son obtains ingenious contrivances (7)
2 Cinema art, and too contrived! (8,7)
3 Some leg of veal (4)
4 Thickness of body (7)
5 Tastes quite enough on board (7)
6 Every topless beach has one (4)
7 Describes it snap badly, a weak character we hear (6,1,8)
8 Eve's hip dislocated makes her irritable (7)
13 Strange evils and disguises (5)
14 Ascetic bear appears before mid-morning (5)
17 Topping Persian fairy to scold (7)
18 Had turned to rock flowers (7)

19 French ruffians cause pain in uppish health resort (7)

20 Soames Forsyte's daughter embraces an idle fellow (7)

24 Not Stevenson's better half (4)

25 Like a man who won at Wimbledon (4)

ACROSS

1 Service providing overhead savings for those in deep water (3,3,6)
8 Articles – a collection of literary anecdotes (3)
9 A popular little paper (7)
11 See about the German left when getting on in years (7)
12 A block which, understandably, is found under a shroud (4-3)
13 Dance around having been thrashed (5)
14 Hides land destroyed by lazy workforce (4,5)
16 Gun AI produced in a lazy way – sluggishly (9)
18 Hymn to a Greek deity each included (5)
20 Liberate one soul in torment (7)
22 Dressed like a lord, while 'is missus went down the pit (7)
23 They educate communities in the main (7)
25 Window at the front of the ship? (3)
26 Press up maybe for a military rehearsal (4,8)

DOWN

1 Leave an orchestra while it's playing (7)
2 No longer working, but unlikely to get a flat (7)
3 Worm-catching communications satellite (5,4)
4 Tailoring trade gets assessed for community charge (5)
5 Day when alumni return to southern university (7)
6 Some of *Ursa Minor*'s debris returns to be seen from Earth by only a few (3)
7 Aquatints? (12)
10 Reprimand for not getting togged up (8,4)
15 One prone to sermonising (3,6)
17 People lifting their heads a lot? In bad golf you find it (7)
18 Remains within easy reach of Naples (7)

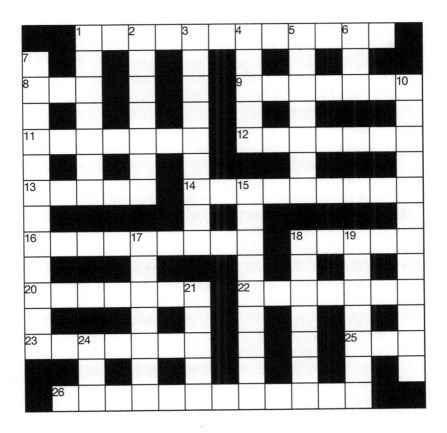

19 Broken bone Len has to raise (7)
21 Some slackness exposed by the cricket team (5)
24 A lady's man by the year's end (3)

ACROSS

1 An amorous street assailant is all confused (6-6)
8 Bowler who tosses up seafood (7)
9 Having members that get engaged? (7)
11 He goes in, as a striker (7)
12 A number of faces around deceptive in appearance (7)
13 Kind of meal at one roughly (5)
14 Frank consumed with desire to be an MP? (9)
16 Constantly accommodating a demanding Oriental (9)
19 French soldier turns up carrying fuel (5)
21 Monotonous drone by the tom-tom (7)
23 Emblematic device used by showman stopping short of Brazilian city (7)
24 Levy by local authority in the red should be newly assessed (7)
25 Feel ill after parties and leave port (3,4)
26 Business procedures requiring resolute action (4,8)

DOWN

1 Area of distribution at Bath I find (7)
2 He admits the FBI agent had some food brought in (7)
3 Peace proposal for the Irish Republic and Northern Ireland initially to study (9)
4 Sawyer rises provided there is a theme (5)
5 One quit bad coaching for a dish of dumplings (7)
6 Chained unruly animal (7)
7 Have a concerted bash to raise money (4,8)
10 Notorious prude is disturbed by statistics chart (12)
15 He believed himself to be winning on the pools! (9)
17 Japanese warrior is imbibing a drink, one knocked back (7)
18 Appearing maturer could be a mistake (7)

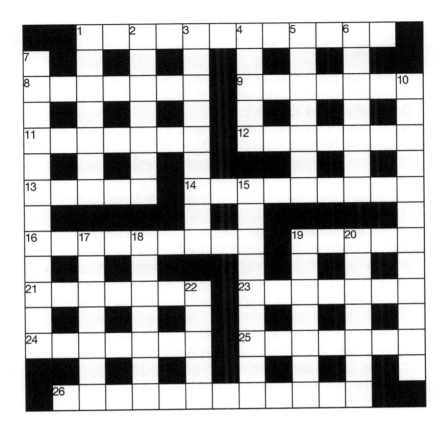

19 Father's sailor is well up in rock charts (3,4)

20 Cold white covers take up space on Channel Island (7)

22 It afflicts picnickers as light turns for example dim (5)

ACROSS

1 Land use affected a tree least (4,6)
6 Wildly hoot German emperor (4)
9 Clique in taxi take a left (5)
10 Moved a bed and table subject to dispute (9)
12 Makers of fine lace and ragged clothing (7)
13 After a short time Ron's a feeble-minded person (5)
15 Gargantuan meal causes spare tyre to be put on (4,3)
17 This art is increasing, people say, in Japan (7)
19 Running may be regarded as smart (7)
21 Own Scottish bay, perhaps, though other horses are found here (7)
22 Nothing in vine is blighted – that's the final word (5)
24 The devil is a most evil fellow (7)
27 Wait, say, on the crossing in Kent (9)
28 Show of unusual entertainment initially (5)
29 The key to a US university (4)
30 Got involved with organising decent ride (10)

DOWN

1 For example, Derby or Redcar's first champion (4)
2 Airborne traveller well below par (9)
3 Story comes up about Conservative leader, with striking effect (5)
4 The best organised flier carries stamps (7)
5 Thanks to well-qualified people, business is hot! (7)
7 Where the Roman tribe settled (5)
8 Ship sunk in lone race (5,5)
11 Plug for an original watchmaker (7)
14 Enid let boy run wild, as ordered (10)
16 Master thespian's one in Dickensian character (7)

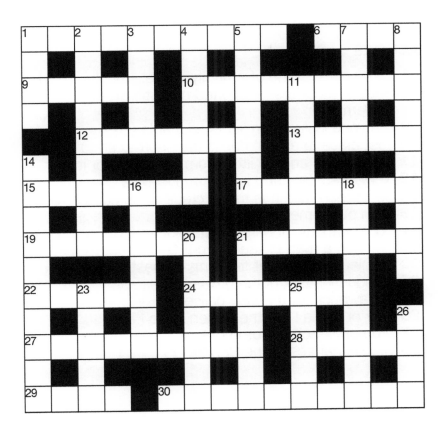

18 Plant in Andorra so exotic (6,3)
20 Give some pleasure to tot in depression (7)
21 Refined dame found in one educational place (7)
23 Open to bribery, but could lean against first (5)
25 Gold I used in current architectural style (5)
26 French fire died in conflict (4)

ACROSS

1 Eventual outcome of a highly successful play (4,3)
5 Baby's father first supported nihilistic art movement (7)
9 Everyone included in list is educable (9)
10 Last place to expect public transport to go to (5)
11 I laze about and do little, from the sound of it (5)
12 Newly-wed hale and hearty in prison (9)
13 Benchmark which is to the credit of detectives (9)
16 I fish out something to sit on (5)
17 Double about...about...about...a duke (5)
18 Fletcher, a man of the church (9)
20 Garbled verse about finishing off pasta (9)
23 Introduction Rex put into verse (5)
25 A drawback for the Irish police (5)
26 Prior or noble I put the Queen on to (7,2)
27 Drop of French perfume (7)
28 Visual changes to the Capitol (7)

DOWN

1 Bubbly set without the right to be so (7)
2 An AIF detachment supplied comforts for the troops (5)
3 Exercises a certain sense in actual practice (9)
4 Plutocrat heard turning down Robert's request (5)
5 Disk Ernie manufactured for an engraver (3,6)
6 Duck stratagem (5)
7 Showmen make mark endlessly with air-conditioning (9)
8 We hear it's the magazine for gossip (7)
14 Programmes of course for ethnic identity (4,5)
15 Performing together (2,7)
16 Indicate where many deposit first in a hole in the wall (4,5)
17 Hurt old mother first (7)

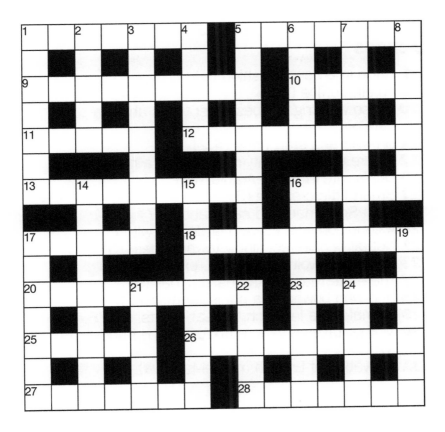

19 So-called lion-man running wild (7)
21 Author produces most of the book (5)
22 It may go by ship and go by car (5)
24 He recorded a hit in *Hamlet* (5)

ACROSS

1 Rude in a gentle fashion (9)
9 Foreign office (6)
10 Those wanting the best offer views about a catalogue (9)
11 Unwrap and start firing (4,2)
12 Where army authority is vested as a rule (2,7)
13 One's fate in Saudi Arabia? (6)
17 Smart little creature (3)
19 Grim Scotsman and sailor about (7)
20 A condition little Edward ended up with (7)
21 Not all people feel kindly towards deer (3)
23 Behold a revolutionary in a Texan town (6)
27 There are many at the bakers' ball (9)
28 One who bowed to a papist woman (6)
29 Formal attire in which to treat hearts, say (5,4)
30 Mother takes a vehicle up for use by bandsman (6)
31 Derivation of English mother-race (9)

DOWN

2 She's a big noise in Tyne and Wear (6)
3 An article to be followed (6)
4 One has no power in banking (6)
5 Clear round called in this game for ladies (7)
6 Too self-important to hit it back to us? There's nothing in it (9)
7 Airmen ate in mess to refresh the body (2-7)
8 Being in wrong groove and getting tied up in a knot causes depravity (9)
14 Deadly weapons babies have (5,4)
15 Vehicle scratched outside – here is the driver's record (5,4)
16 Once round the rose-garden that is in submission (9)

17 Charge costs nothing – not right (3)
18 Animal little Kathleen brought up (3)
22 Lily supporting party banner (7)
24 The union that speaks with one voice (6)
25 Have a bet about ass, you dog (6)
26 Less than half are psychotic! (6)

ACROSS

1 Polaris calls for old PM's seaman (5,4)

9 No-one's sore coming back from a rubbing down (7)

10 Make an impressive design in blue maybe but it is only superficial (7)

11 Lakes 'e'd transformed in the Lake District (7)

12 Guard reading orders with little hesitation (9)

14 Gymnasium event finishes poor people on them (4,4)

15 A plant to tantalise the novice (6)

17 They not only rouse up the game, they win (7)

20 Starry part of a fast rally (6)

23 Tagged onto boy holding beautiful girl (8)

25 Intent, would you say, this daring young man? (9)

26 Looking lecherously despite reeling drunkenly (7)

27 Let about nine mess around, because too forgiving (7)

28 Lack the cause of that fonder feeling (7)

29 He's not at home in the Highlands (9)

DOWN

2 A corny royal refuge! (3,4)

3 Eat nuts in a stew, and illness will result (7)

4 He had scattered clues round the table (8)

5 Venerate Paul the US rebel from the sound of it (6)

6 Appear unkempt to view an officers' club (4,1,4)

7 Type of verse will point at Ulster axis's retreat (7)

8 How a royal warrant is given to protect the chassis from rust (5,4)

13 Everyday withdrawal of currency (7)

15 But this extension of the board does not come off in Autumn (5,4)

16 Expedition leader with phoney bulletin is boiling over (9)

18 The spirited character of a nicer sort of ship? (8)

19 Be a star performing side by side (7)

21 Multi-storey hotel in a European city (7)

22 Revised scenario has no love, merely poison (7)

24 Sharp-eyed birds in golf-holes (6)

ACROSS

4 Fighting an opponent of it (8)
8 Girl bitter back in the European capital (6)
9 Where films may be exposed and crimes unheard of (2,6)
10 John and I can give up the job (4,2,2)
11 Kidnap the sailor by the canal (6)
12 Seems mad to order married ladies abroad! (8)
13 Taking trouble to point out (8)
16 The writing is on the wall (8)
19 Jokes I rarely made about Liberal leader (8)
21 Where merry men lay down for a kip, we hear (6)
23 A painter gets out more when the weather's fine (8)
24 The state of this carriage! (8)
25 African animals originating from eastern countries (6)
26 Has ordered factory-made walking stick (8)

DOWN

1 Dim-sighted King in bed (7)
2 Checked – and upbraided (6,3)
3 Record time in completion of partition (6)
4 Makes up face with oils? (6,1,8)
5 Whale said to be worth a considerable amount (8)
6 Celebrated mother's return and had a meal out (5)
7 Knighted colonel turns to company getting the wind up (7)
14 Extension for dining (5,4)
15 A climbing plant – in need of air, it was (8)
17 Bird that is seen first by raw recruits (7)
18 Awful cad sure to organise a militant campaign (7)

20 I'm about to stay in the same place (6)
22 Bar in which poets may be found (5)

ACROSS

1 A girl medic trained in antiseptic function (10)
6 Spirit of Kay in endless wet weather (4)
10 Persons entitled to make money in listening devices (5)
11 Changed bit of mineral could harm a prop (9)
12 Lanky individual supporting runners (4,4)
13 An old curiosity like a knot (5)
15 Can be seen nearing disaster (2,5)
17 Vulnerable to a point of issue (7)
19 Miserable one abroad, a dwarf (7)
21 *The World Needs Love* performed on this lute? (7)
22 Peg will not quite succeed (5)
24 Claim ale could have been spilt on the flower (8)
27 Stay to eat and drink (9)
28 Grit found in dinner vegetables (5)
29 Journey before fall? (4)
30 Drink with card-game takes the biscuit (6,4)

DOWN

1 North Briton hears the wind (4)
2 Element from fine soil (4,5)
3 He wrote *Ben is Reformed* (5)
4 Beg for an MP to have knowledge (7)
5 Stuffy order not to talk about so much... (7)
7 ...made less stuffy by Edward's demeanour (5)
8 I make Henry go into the country for inspiration (10)
9 A people with the necessary power ready to co-operate (8)
14 £51 rise, perhaps, should get one a kitchen-appliance (10)
16 Emperor's gold coin (8)
18 Nobleman, that is to say Ronald previously (7,2)
20 Bemused Tracey about an hour with a sailor (7)

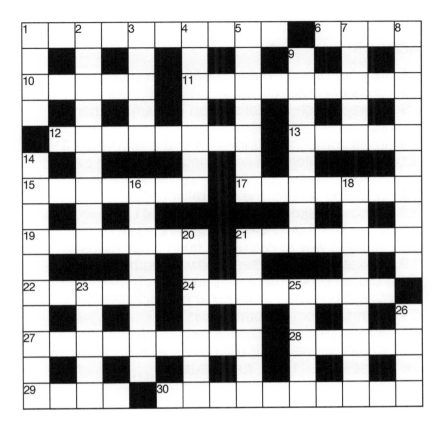

21 Squirrel-monkey in the river first (7)
23 Damaged pew I'd gone over with a duster (5)
25 The French name Kay heartlessly as being awkwardly tall (5)
26 One old car in a pile-up (4)

ACROSS

1 Kept out of sight but enticed Kay in (6)
5 Tubes of paste (8)
9 Where Danish capitalists can be found at home? (10)
10 Ship's company sounded off in the farmyard (4)
11 Such poisoning has he-cat in agony, going to earth (8)
12 Australian port for the naturalist (6)
13 Unknown traitor about to declaim (4)
15 Pictures of fully-developed six-footers (8)
18 Finding a way to call up is quite touching (8)
19 Relaxation in Battersea's Edwardian homes (4)
21 A discarded garment worn in Spain (6)
23 What a batsman must do to be a success (4,1,3)
25 Bill of fare for acceptable bills! (4)
26 Fanciful pieces of soaps hired out (10)
27 Does one have a big bill, having let out clutch? (8)
28 Braise served up in Yugoslavia (6)

DOWN

2 About-turn for a submarine (1-4)
3 Sharp encounter between professional mourners? (4,5)
4 Hilda is upset over a bloomer (6)
5 An attractive pointer (8,7)
6 A countryman is able to aid an organisation (8)
7 Le Mans driver in car – one designed for speed (5)
8 Nine seeds germinating in dearth? (9)
14 Justice for a goodly number (1,4,4)
16 You hear I slander a man from Reykjavik (9)
17 Hair style for a school's annual turn-out (4,4)
20 Arbitrary commands, for the sake of change in America (6)
22 Haggard father of the House of Lancaster (5)

24 Old people confined to bed want nice nightwear (5)

ACROSS

1 Better from Maesteg, right? (8)
5 Be right on the heels of the big man (6)
9 Support scouting group by providing hiking equipment (4,4)
10 Big run on a famous Swiss bank (6)
12 Utter base calumny then hide (3,3)
13 It could be set at your place, or mine (5,3)
15 Hounds chasing black birds (7)
16 A French firm is remarkable in Scotland (4)
20 See what's written concerning publicity (4)
21 Silly man sometimes? (7)
25 Fortune-teller accepts old money for David (8)
26 Trophy for champion layer? (3,3)
28 Smear some of this mud generally in (6)
29 A stirring call for military personnel (8)
30 News of the overseas cricket match (6)
31 In the Piedmontese capital Kelly retired (6,2)

DOWN

1 Indistinct speech coming from bachelor with a follower in the wind (6)
2 This Finn could knock out a mouse (6)
3 Imagined having had some food, so upset inside (8)
4 Eat out in style, though it stretches resources (4)
6 Way to go round on foot (6)
7 A simple brain makes for a clear conscience (4,4)
8 Drawing an old engine (8)
11 Man leaves a German to enter cathedral city with enthusiasm (7)
14 Once more a righteous man is in opposition (7)
17 Support also arranged for the suggested plan (8)
18 Weed killer some spread around water (8)
19 The writer going around to match a colour (3-5)

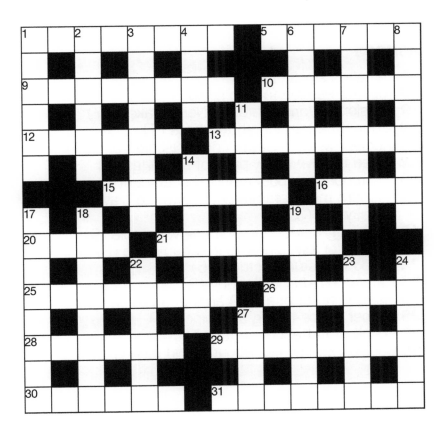

22 Game is arranged for such pictures (6)
23 Climbed up in an hierarchical system (6)
24 It modifies the blood and may be vent (6)
27 A lover of attractive women – but no ties! (4)

ACROSS

1 He takes stock (7)
5 Topping Persian fairy to scold (7)
9 Sessions of drinks around North Dakota (7)
10 A paper pattern length for dress (7)
11 Indolent workers Satan finds mischief for (4,5)
12 Opted to have many pairs of stockings (5)
13 To pronounce about craft is impertinent (5)
15 Its team members are not allowed to play in the penalty-box (3,6)
17 Invert sugar added to a spring vegetable (9)
19 An area of low rainfall is in a bad state (5)
22 Is about to study pictures (5)
23 Harry goes after dollar dog (9)
25 Instrument for aria NCO arranged (7)
26 Former prince taking a province (7)
27 Plainly smart about status (7)
28 Gossips with stories about island race (7)

DOWN

1 Trying members of the courts (7)
2 Tickets for a Wimbledon match maybe (7)
3 General chief physician of old (5)
4 Being displeased about note sent, telephone (9)
5 Rings friends – there's point in that (5)
6 Strike a number with financial liabilities as extortionate (9)
7 A wizard music man! (7)
8 Balcony which Rex installed in the main kitchen (7)
14 Benchmark which is to the credit of detectives (9)
16 Where Great Yarmouth is teas cost a bomb (4,5)
17 Not quite all there? That's rather unfair (1,3,3)
18 Sailor turning up in Malayan boat is well-proportioned (3,4)
20 Indifferent car is not in gear (7)

21 They come from the north and south of the country (7)
23 Alert enough to live for a day out (5)
24 Custom-wear? (5)

ACROSS

1 With drooping tubular bloomers, one says very little at factory (6,5)
9 Where one travels in the course of a safari (4)
10 One out on his feet? (5,6)
11 In the hedge another wild cherry (4)
14 Worry about a proverb that cuts across the grain (4,3)
16 Swimmer with a deep voice? (3,4)
17 In general a German product... (5)
18 Shocking swimmers? (4)
19 Photographed attempt at goal (4)
20 When they do cyclists must step on it (5)
22 Nail that is ready initially is rather more sticky (7)
23 Little room in no Scottish aircraft enclosure (7)
24 Dog and dog-end (4)
28 Everybody, say, with alternative I state to be symbolic (11)
29 Sound from *Animal Farm*, Orwell's first writing material (4)
30 Melted fat, about a pint for make-up (6,5)

DOWN

2 Only Alexandria contains a famous university (4)
3 Arrangement of late carrying weight in China (4)
4 Stripped pine needs harsh treatment (3,4)
5 Lie about a lolly with its end bitten off (4)
6 Comparatively very poor (7)
7 What a relief, being freed later (5,6)
8 Leaning, dog is a pacemaker (5,6)
12 Pretence at being in love (11)
13 Light diversions? (11)
15 Mass nourishment, although only a light snack (5)
16 *Danse Macabre* in American saloon (5)
20 This diver is outstandingly good down under (7)

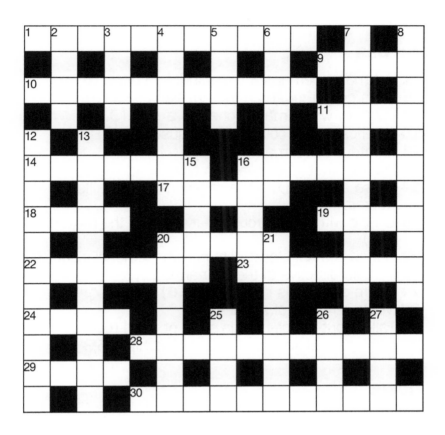

21 Sugar extracted from alecost (7)
25 Plea to woman from orphan's platform (4)
26 Popular singer keen to make a come back (4)
27 In mid America English find a French city (4)

ACROSS

1 Put many, perhaps a thousand, in a drum (8)
5 Seas do get rough on the Russian coast (6)
9 Vulgarity which makes one pull a face (3,5)
10 American dupe collapsed, exhausted (4,2)
11 Amateur bandsman? (5,3)
12 Idle talk that gives blimpish types a lift (3,3)
14 Those seeing to travel arrangements for skilled workers? (10)
18 Engine with dirt in trouble – it's part of the mixture (10)
22 One in Los Angeles, California who is not clerical (6)
23 Intrepid directive to the over-anxious (8)
24 Sharp-eyed birds in golf-holes (6)
25 Made rare sort of sugar (8)
26 Talk about a fool, not his state of mind (6)
27 Intimate and secure blood relationship? (5,3)

DOWN

1 A knightly habit, thanks to Shakespeare (6)
2 Managed, with difficulty, a successful party (4,2)
3 Flower of a fighting woman (6)
4 Consult Ria, discovering about sound waves (10)
6 Find a record superior (8)
7 Weapons never used at the front? (4,4)
8 Discernible as a quiet Mum, for instance (8)
13 Zestful hint of Sir Robert's allegiance to William III (6,4)
15 If retired, senior chaps have positions at Lord's (8)
16 Encouraging egg-nog in whisked form (6,2)
17 Perverse as insurgent Jack in depression (8)
19 Item of clothing barristers hope to acquire (6)
20 Old teacher panted terribly (6)
21 Prisoner's welcome break? (6)

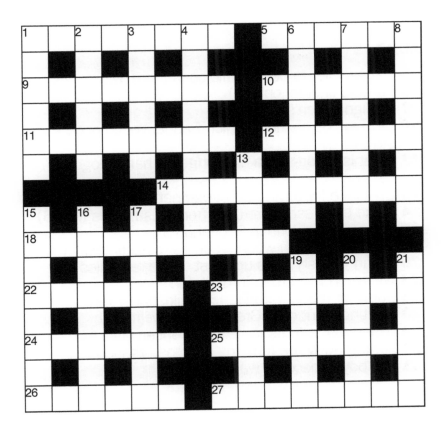

ACROSS

5 Forces valet to be a comic character (6)
8 Put into liquidation? (8)
9 Foreign legion's drink (4,3)
10 Old Tayside castle in which Raquel Welch once stayed (5)
11 What is a-dog-and-a-half long and half-a-dog high? (9)
13 Dry place for driving off altogether (8)
14 Make effervescent return after a disastrous tea (6)
17 I take one for John in Scotland (3)
19 Without a match when it comes to eccentricity (3)
20 Italian dynasty uses up most of the remedies (6)
23 Writer dipping bread in drink (8)
26 Outfit for model with French philosopher (9)
28 Starting point on a Great Lake is weird (5)
29 Loving, but admits to being a conservative (7)
30 Putting away the remains in some irritation (8)
31 The boy to become warden (6)

DOWN

1 Most attractive road in Mediterranean resort (6)
2 Blow £1! (7)
3 Therefore, put no male in charge of work study (9)
4 Where little David returns in North America (6)
5 This produces no capital growth naturally (4,4)
6 Note the false incisors (5)
7 Put off by article about rest, scoffed (8)
12 A small weight on the vestment (3)
15 Looked on as a bloomer by people in the Alps (9)
16 Inebriated chaps those Sherwood Foresters (5,3)
18 A frenzy of war cries and whirling blades (3-5)
21 Greek letter and French article (3)
22 It is clear that rail services have been cancelled (2,5)

24 Apply friction to a discord to be played with a flexible tempo (6)

25 Come out for Oriental associate (6)

27 State rank (5)

ACROSS

1 Local attendants prohibit bids (10)
9 Note and second note (4)
10 Wind it down for the season! (10)
11 Has got into a sports car dumbfounded (6)
12 Darlings of modern music makers? (7)
15 Rock 'n' roll player? The latter certainly (7)
16 Each decimal base has presumably been chewed over (5)
17 501 freshwater fish (4)
18 Antitoxins found right in the ocean (4)
19 Captured, we hear, where they played tennis (5)
21 Where to find someone having difficulties (2,1,4)
22 Hankered for months to join Edward (7)
24 Lament of the first King George and the first lady (6)
27 Control and cheat a labourer (4,2,4)
28 Some darts pro cheats, by overstepping this line? (4)
29 Use real care in creating a healthier atmosphere (7,3)

DOWN

2 Summit unknown to primate at first (4)
3 2 x 2! (6)
4 Hurried back with speed to give account of events (7)
5 Vile, bad and very unpleasant (4)
6 A youngster surrounded by 5 anti-Crusader (7)
7 Instruction to hurry at chess? (3,1,4,2)
8 Smuggled goods to Nicaraguan guerrilla group (10)
12 Stuffing not replaced on bear (10)
13 What aggressive manager does for boxer (4,1,5)

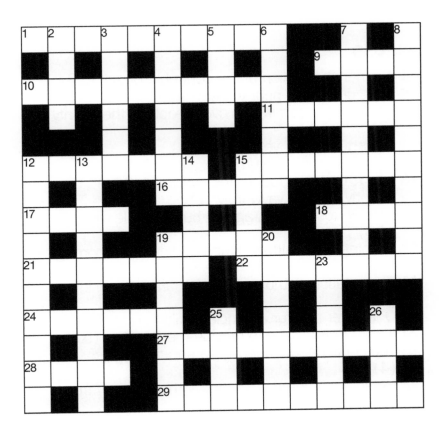

14 Something afoot when the boat's capsized (5)
15 Snoop round hesitantly for a drink (5)
19 Sulphur not found in make-up of heavenly body (7)
20 Sent packing before Number One returns suffering from strain (7)
23 Bacon could be comparatively audacious (6)
25 This Scottish isle is heaven, people say (4)
26 In at making a contrary suggestion (4)

ACROSS

1 Nunnery has a lion under control? Correct! (12)
9 Drag one's feet prior to dealing (7)
10 Endless row coming up over people in the county (7)
11 Departed or not yet arrived? (4)
12 From Cremona I returned exalted (2,3)
13 Can it turn the tide for the overweight? (4)
16 Silently, cattily, waywardly (7)
17 Crosby upset about ageing but valuable writer (4,3)
18 Nothing at breakfast, lunch or dinner but porridge (7)
21 Exclamation of those central characters taking a girl (7)
23 One silver ring for an ancient mind-poisoner (4)
24 It's up to a painter to provide the jewellery (5)
25 Top-class deputy head gave unbeatable service (4)
28 Hotspur's leaders score first – there's a cry from the field (5-2)
29 Ann could be enthusiastic with the material (7)
30 Put one's name to a hire purchase contract? (5,2,5)

DOWN

1 Cuts possibly made about one in charge are severe (7)
2 Crass f-football follower stands on his head (4)
3 Where the cross peer got a denial in France (7)
4 Checking to see if the fare is all right (7)
5 Dummies found in ruined sofa (4)
6 With hidden energy, Ali on a restored harp (7)
7 Monroe supporters say NATO's oil is its undoing (13)

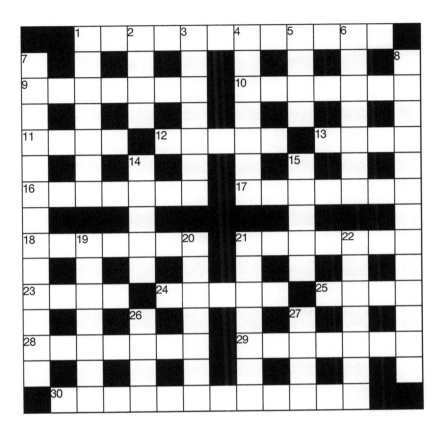

8 Blade entering ship is fun for kids (13)
14 Unfairly 'e hurt Arthur's Dad (5)
15 Pound up a street with dynamite (5)
19 Language used to label a record (7)
20 Prepared for an awkward guy getting outside help (4,3)
21 John Peel crazy for seedy fruit? (4-3)
22 The heart of the matter (7)
26 The sound of jive can reduce one to hobbling (4)
27 Row back in a knot (4)

ACROSS

7 Punish one of the seven dwarfs for being careless? (4,5)

8 Study the art of beer drinking? (3,2)

10 The pineapple, long fruit with the top removed (6)

11 Are changing part, part of the telephone (3,5)

12 Evil article on a war peninsula (6)

14 Higher residential area now put out (6)

16 Regretfully, a girl lost a shilling (4)

17 In modern times anger is publicly displayed (5)

18 Appropriate at the present time (4)

19 Third party providing proper guarantee in Spain (6)

21 True, an exceptional character (6)

24 One real tug can make it binding (8)

26 First letter opened by a Philistine city girl (6)

27 After dodging bail I found an excuse (5)

28 Make cuts, that's what customers of a disobliging fishmonger did (5,4)

DOWN

1 Dressing after midnight brings a sparkle (5)

2 Welcome order for riflemen waiting for weapon inspection (4,4)

3 Light wood with head of match for relief from cold (6)

4 Record the same note twice – it's sharp (4)

5 He's barely human (6)

6 Bed-frame for marriage partners (5,4)

9 There's a revolution on all sides (6)

13 A body of gunmen turned on him (5)

15 Seemingly reasonable it might make Bill pause (9)

17 A hundred in a coach. You can count on it (6)

18 Cartoons to display on a festive occasion! (8)

20 Close – doubly close in fact (6)

22 Plant provided meals, as reported, the French conclude (6)

23 Wrap for a writer over 50 (5)

25 Eat out, and so on at Hindhead (4)

21

ACROSS

1 Learn a craft? He's bound to (10)
9 Arab prince recalls Ancient Mariner's story (4)
10 The scale of EEC trading abroad (10)
11 Arrive to put a map away? (4,2)
12 Messenger has a job getting in beer (7)
15 Belt on smart bluebottle (7)
16 Give up interest in shares (5)
17 Secures inconclusive results (4)
18 The charge is about right, but you don't have to pay (4)
19 Legal actions? (5)
21 Smarter French painter (7)
22 Listeners burning to get within hearing distance (7)
24 Place of secret laughter (6)
27 Transfix with sword in rehearsal (3-7)
28 A school setting the tone (4)
29 Club gets convict into hellish trouble (10)

DOWN

2 Look for exercise record (4)
3 A trio's broken relationships (6)
4 Regularly late? Yet sounding chivalrous (7)
5 Outbreak of rain in the country (4)
6 Gemstone – a dealer maybe holds a number (7)
7 Quite enough out of school (10)
8 An early settlement (10)
12 Staggers, due to ill-fitting satin shoes (10)
13 Too far into no-man's land? (4,3,3)
14 Dis duck – or dat? (5)
15 It cuts a dashing figure (5)
19 Wastes the rewards (7)
20 The case for school books (7)
23 Train for Rugby, for example (6)

25 He's against the proposal and ain't going to change! (4)

26 Eager to work in silver (4)

ACROSS

1 Barber's reduced charge? (3-5)
5 Compel me to include this device above the curtains (6)
10 Is it wrong for him to be unhappy? (9,6)
11 The said container father had in the capital (7)
12 Gareth not taking the trouble to come down with some flowers (7)
13 Deliberate swindle by partisan (8)
15 Many a seagull from Scotland flying round the parrot (5)
18 Bill has a set of exam questions (5)
20 Associate employee gets behind the firm (2-6)
23 Policeman at workplace encounters little resistance (7)
25 Used rag haphazardly that had been coated with a sweet substance (7)
26 Royal Oak? (4,2,3,6)
27 Despite being difficult is having a go (6)
28 Finish in the finish shut in (8)

DOWN

1 Acquire pass (4,2)
2 Squad going after a job for the working party (4-5)
3 Rose-red letters arranged on the screen (7)
4 Be getting in something to chew cut up (5)
6 Mince pie has little weight according to the saying (7)
7 Miraculous food mother gives girl getting up (5)
8 Reject request to reduce the volume (4,4)
9 Bushes in a straight line on the boundary? (8)
14 'e first cut up Art Deco wallpaper (8)
16 Gloomy supporters do this when their team is less successful (9)
17 Tooth in a wheel – put pair in hollow receptacle (8)

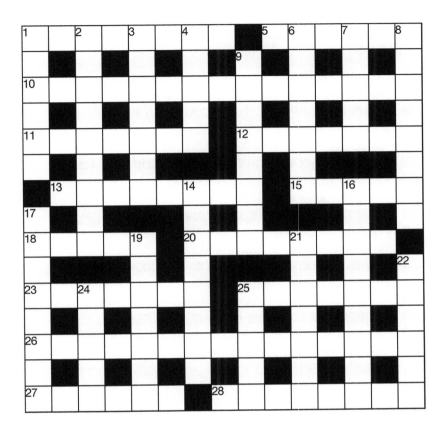

19 Coco ran wild, the beast (7)
21 Slattern's toy? (7)
22 New diet Edward prepared (6)
24 It's ornate, just imagine (5)
25 Back at sea, it's grim (5)

23

ACROSS

5 A winger, a Greek character, gone berserk (6)
8 Provided only of the same size (2,4,2)
9 Shops keep one for the accounts (7)
10 Give instruction to a pirate (5)
11 Fair to all – beer's ordered (9)
13 Military personnel, proficient yet withdrawn (8)
14 Spoil a naughty child to show off (6)
17 Tell for instance (3)
19 One's not entirely irreplaceable! (3)
20 A quarter lock – emphasise that (6)
23 Invalids involved in pain test (8)
26 Paid attention after midnight, and looked bright (9)
28 Saying take little notice with advancing years (5)
29 Managed to continue making capital (7)
30 Governor who's grim about rocky situation (8)
31 Tasted awful, so it's claimed (6)

DOWN

1 Entranced over golden eagle (6)
2 A variety of gravel found in Portugal (7)
3 The woman all on her own from choice (9)
4 Article framed by shrewd old king (6)
5 Deplorable way to call for retirement (8)
6 Edgar's rebellious girl (5)
7 Covered or left face-up? (8)
12 No minister may appear eccentric (3)
15 Brought together about a hundred on drugs (9)
16 Set out to entrap law-breaking firm (8)
18 A type of hormone that builds a heavenly body (8)
21 An animal living in the sea perhaps (3)
22 The youngster presented to a princess (7)
24 A good-looker, a big shot in the underworld, holding on (6)

25 Blunder in shamefaced to get a drink (6)
27 Sense this would be a great deal (5)

ACROSS

1 Gift of old money (6)
4 Brutish affected manners, say, of privateers (8)
9 Round the navy, tea is served in fancy style (6)
10 Smooth and cheerful on air-bed, perhaps (8)
12 Mail goes astray in capital (4)
13 Some prehistoric reptiles crawled on all fours (5)
14 Total power where oil is found (4)
17 Early carriage propelled by generator? (12)
20 Book showing currant-cake, one as set out (12)
23 Design of factory incomplete? (4)
24 Scope of morning-piece (5)
25 Creature dead, with nothing to follow? You can say that again! (4)
28 Noble trio of Beethoven (8)
29 Einstein, for example, using energy in formula (6)
30 List of terms giving polish to a line (8)
31 Test of gold leading to bargain? (6)

DOWN

1 English writer seen in baggage-point (8)
2 Nelson's column, for example, makes impression underground (8)
3 Sign register (4)
5 Potter's way of keeping advantage (12)
6 Backward-flying owls (4)
7 Such endless air-trouble he had, coming unstuck (6)
8 Thinly-spread butter for pickle (6)
11 Ringleader in remote Kabul, going around as a rabble-rouser (12)
15 Smell of a fishing-vessel (5)
16 This row goes on endlessly, we hear (5)
18 Poison derived from a protein (8)

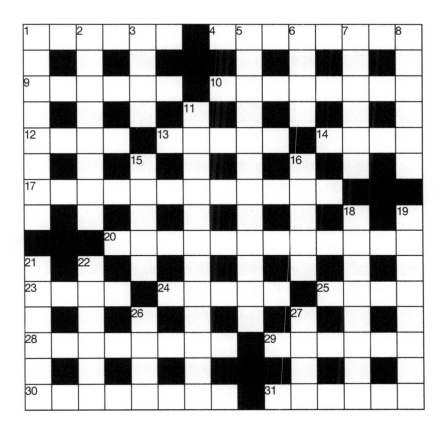

19 Support for displaced Poles, going around America (8)
21 Bounded from singular accident? (6)
22 Argentinian suffering a cough (6)
26 Bad time for Caesar in squalid escapade (4)
27 Last in river? (4)

25

ACROSS

7 Go on! Take a holiday! (3,4)
8 Liberal in charge shows character (7)
10 Canal worker unaffected by alopecia (4-6)
11 Instant credit (4)
12 Turtle placed quietly in the ground (8)
14 Poems by salvationists in the Ukraine (6)
15 Reprimanded for having been driven to work (5,2,4)
19 Compensate by offering cosmetics (4,2)
20 Tubby lad retaliates in anger (6,2)
22 Not all the best etymologists use original words (4)
23 Long thought to be a mirror image (10)
25 Relative runs into trouble (7)
26 A bogus pressman should be mortified (7)

DOWN

1 After public protest Edward was downgraded (7)
2 Support for the spine (4)
3 Agree to raise the hem (4,2)
4 Made curator admit variable conduct (5,3)
5 I had returned strained and upset (10)
6 Quite right to adapt recipes (7)
9 He certainly doesn't lay out cash with caution (11)
13 Earl renovated English country property (4,6)
16 Foreign trader is no longer stout (8)
17 Charge producer for assault (7)
18 Lad swallows single humbug (7)
21 A French midshipman is apprehensive (6)
24 Squad takes note in the morning (4)

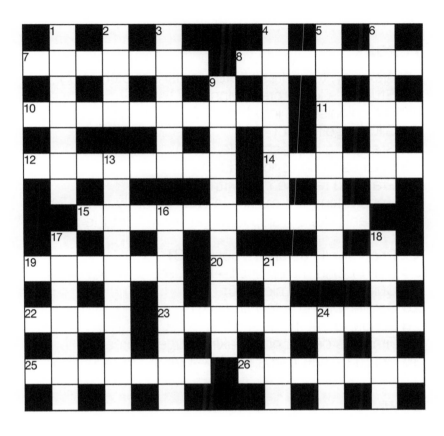

26

ACROSS

1 Alex, say, to undress before artist's sketch (5,7)
9 Student's left a breadwinner (7)
10 Old colonist put into the earth next to monarch (7)
11 Slice a golf shot (4)
12 Started to request article (5)
13 Useless to be conceited (4)
16 Prayer to replace gale with sun (7)
17 Keep taking the mickey in West Country town (7)
18 Volcanic ridge – ship is to get away from the point (7)
21 Pride swells as one is born (4,3)
23 Don't begin magic spell – it causes damage (4)
24 Quietly press to clear out (5)
25 Soldier writing a few lines (4)
28 Period to eat in? Yes! (3-4)
29 Firm has deficit, one making huge figures (7)
30 Henman, say, earns plenty – I must struggle (6,6)

DOWN

1 Working hard and investing retained money (7)
2 Called to the bar (4)
3 Colour of America's hero of old (7)
4 Poisoner to stop using petroleum derivative (7)
5 Neckwear said to be Asian (4)
6 Reject unpopular actors (7)
7 Once television was admitting no compromise? (5-3-5)
8 Unsympathetic advice to one in painful labour? (4,3,4,2)
14 Insinuating ships have capsized (5)
15 Coach's expression of annoyance with men (5)
19 Through which a beggar sorts? (7)
20 Crockery may be flying (7)

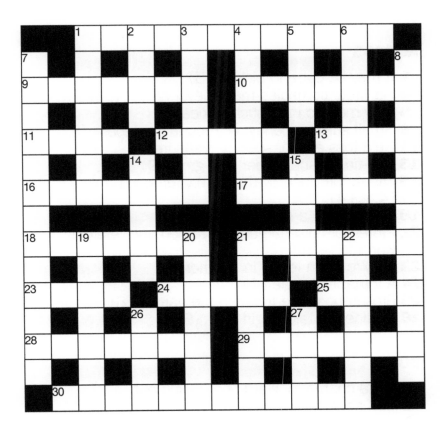

21 American soldier is in the pub – that's reasonable (7)

22 Fast horse, we hear, is not so well bred (7)

26 Not quite wonderful North European (4)

27 Announce liberal arrested for murder (4)

ACROSS

1 It may be cut and pickled (5)
4 He wrote comedies many never go out to see (8)
8 Only men go in at such a meeting (8)
9 Small sum of money sent round as deposit (8)
11 He'd toss a coin, seeking pleasure (7)
13 Rag-time band leader was great (9)
15 Tribute provided by the gallery for inborn talent? (4,4,3,4)
18 Took part in a dramatic trial (9)
21 Professors discharged – ie retired and retaining worth (7)
22 They're often found in a lather (8)
24 A romantic tangle (4,4)
25 Broken boot-tree found in the garden (8)
26 Declined to take a girl back (5)

DOWN

1 Not a charge for wardrobe equipment (4,6)
2 Fruit no good for pudding (4,4)
3 Russian family rule that came to an end in a revolutionary way (8)
4 New cost of baby beds (4)
5 Tax-protester who presented her buff form (6)
6 Outpace former top tennis player, we hear (6)
7 Issue of an American magazine turned up (4)
10 There's a regular stream at day's end (8)
12 Many were awoken when people had a drunken party (8)
14 Limited form of credit provided after period of unemployment (10)
16 Insect with wings of short span (8)
17 I plan too haphazardly but it's a matter of choice (8)
19 Cast ashore? That's rough (6)

20 A news broadcast with right to reply (6)
22 He continues to work for southern transport (4)
23 An opening possibly lost (4)

ACROSS

1 Richard from Middle East initially had a leguminous plant (6)
4 Showy shooter a photographer uses? (8)
10 College girl in town (5,4)
11 Pleased name had been included for part of the body (5)
12 Second sailor scrubbing on rest-day (7)
13 Figure of eight (7)
14 Was early, yes indeed almost (5)
15 Display plumage in a confrontation (8)
18 Study the battle for a starter (8)
20 Singular item of clothing from New York left on (5)
23 Case for the government (7)
25 Bloomer ie safer to reproduce (7)
26 Cover all but the start of the season (5)
27 Still employing or wearing (7,2)
28 These orders herald a dismissal (8)
29 Uncomfortable and hard presumably (6)

DOWN

1 You will be certain if you do this (4,4)
2 During the wedding, battled to find an eccentric person from North America (7)
3 Accountant Stanley set out to find an instrument (9)
5 Luckily come down the right way up? (4,2,4,4)
6 Lot to see (5)
7 Confused gals go west to the city (7)
8 Anne I'd confused with another girl (6)
9 Similarly using an identical symbol (2,3,4,5)
16 Bloomer perpetrated by Daniel and Don perhaps (9)
17 Unwieldy and ugly in an awful way (8)
19 Does it move in high circles? (7)

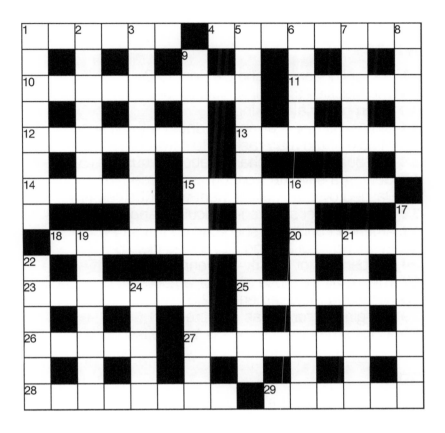

21 Pasta prepared by Alan going round sink (7)
22 Breach of faith? (6)
24 The prime minister got the point (5)

29

ACROSS

1 The delinquent macho element (10)
6 The blackleg's small vehicle for hire (4)
10 Given material backing (5)
11 Single-minded – arranging dates with all speed (9)
12 Middle-of-the-road fashion to consider (8)
13 The board plan to change about a quarter (5)
15 Getting a sailor to work out when free (7)
17 Passed over, so quickly went without sleep (7)
19 Note slimmer's more immaculate appearance (7)
21 American politician shedding no tears (7)
22 Egghead, age around 50, a high-flier (5)
24 Suspension of a Turk – an engineer (8)
27 They're all for those who like a good hot pot! (3-6)
28 Agreed to make amends (2,3)
29 The girl's in for it – as expected (4)
30 A craftsman maybe means to take issue (10)

DOWN

1 Spot a breakwater (4)
2 Gun sale to provide the wherewithal to obtain tasty food (9)
3 Sweet nonsense (5)
4 Downfall of a rogue in a suit (7)
5 Unity makes no sense (7)
7 Links with tea at home (5)
8 The struggle to serve again is a racket! (10)
9 These days work into shape for a take-over (8)
14 City men – the cars possibly show it (10)
16 A knight cut the crowd (8)
18 Express a preference that's made perfectly clear (3,6)
20 A down-to-earth guy in the matter of a catalogue (7)
21 Makes a move over one of the family (7)

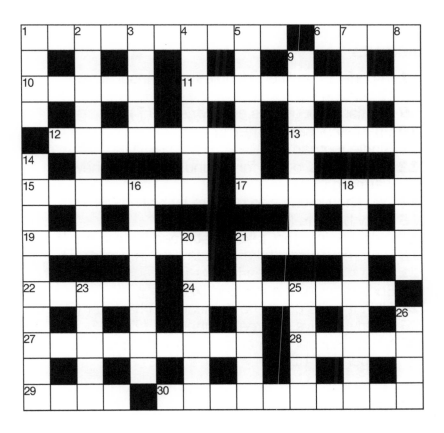

23 Gardening job which is really hard labour (5)
25 A trainee member's fear (5)
26 The writer has a point, Friend! (4)

30

ACROSS

1 In perfect condition, doubles as a nasal-spray (2,5,2,1,4)
9 Cautious about it as endowment? (7)
10 Spanish basket-game? (7)
11 Single footpad? (4)
12 Farmer opts, oddly, for groundsheets that never warm up (10)
14 Two short months to prepare by boiling (6)
15 Nutty biscuits (8)
17 A doctor, in a trip, takes a stringed instrument (8)
18 Hairdresser, say, takes a little time in battle (6)
21 Rock music in the early days (6,4)
22 Endlessly sad run in cloud (4)
24 Ali in it turns out to be the leading character (7)
25 Elderly relative of Greek orphan-girl (7)
26 Naples sunset – an extraordinary, disagreeable happening? (14)

DOWN

1 One brought up to be blamed (7)
2 Fellow-lodger and constant friend (6,9)
3 University head can upset system (4)
4 Uninteresting study of English poet (6)
5 Fig-tree in my care, so unusual (8)
6 Sponsor's caber often tossed? (10)
7 Stumble and go broke? (4,4,7)
8 Does one land on a wing and a prayer? (6)
13 One of three little maids of a certain class (10)
16 Blair is a new name in capital (8)
17 Alarm bell we hear is harmful to us (6)
19 Sailor achieves ambitions (7)
20 Problem in game-plan (6)
23 Role played in average time (4)

31

ACROSS

1 Lard once used in the kitchen (8)

9 Popular king enters love affair ready to fight (2,6)

10 One embraced by the woman's successor (4)

11 Confidentially, the stylus is out of action (3,3,6)

13 Fawn and ram on higher ground (6,2)

15 A stubborn fellow takes time to display charm (6)

16 About to find a fairy (4)

17 Many a girl has style (5)

18 Some of them negotiate a reasonable rent (4)

20 The acid test for literature and music (6)

21 High Churchman wanting God's favour (3,5)

23 When seraphim assembled in state (3,9)

26 Typical measures by crazy people (4)

27 An Italian with one poem for all mankind (8)

28 Rory can't possibly be perverse (8)

DOWN

2 Conspicuous union leader about to make proposal (8)

3 Victory song put on by the victor (3,2,7)

4 Idiot acquires counterfeit sovereign (6)

5 In the Kalahari chameleons are abundant (4)

6 Just habits familiar to golfers (8)

7 Record nothing but a trademark (4)

8 Managing director to whom one is indebted (8)

12 Oppose general direction taken by a singer (7-5)

14 Steal and cook fish? (5)

16 Sententious character of old explorer retiring in America (8)

17 Price paid by woman for aromatic plant (8)

19 Forbear to make an escort distressed (8)

22 Loafer dressed in a petticoat (4-2)

24 Nick has to administer a beating (4)

25 Gamble on finding a small monocle (4)

32

ACROSS

1 Wait a moment, I am accompanied by Pooh (4,4,2)

6 The part of the world of Cambodia, Siam, etc (4)

9 Old boy, see, appallingly overweight (5)

10 The glare of publicity? (9)

12 Choosing a piece of music that's very cheap (5,3,1,4)

14 Panama making war – that's terrible (5,3)

15 One that's out of place, if turned round in fog (6)

17 Point to school we're about to avoid (6)

19 Computer programs frequently conflict in two points (8)

21 How soft bridle broke, where Richard was desperate for a horse (8,5)

24 A piece intended, they say, to be flat (9)

25 Block part of ear (5)

26 Take one from seven – result is divisible by two (4)

27 Gripping film about shopping? (6-4)

DOWN

1 Either way it's a mistake (4)

2 One retaliating may affirm engineer has been captured (7)

3 Continually only half time at the office? (4,2,4,3)

4 Urgent message – great elm has fallen (8)

5 Voodoo priestess will need a doctor in a second (5)

7 Declare unfit, so stop broadcasting (4,3)

8 Singer to win over woman entirely (10)

11 Bound to be ignorant of the consequences of this? (4,2,3,4)

13 Process of collecting lab message has gone wrong (10)

16 The paper that covered the happy couple? (8)

18 Despicable type in protective cover for downpour (7)

20 Cockney to transfer from Hampshire town (7)

22 Force one may show in rows? (5)

23 Cut speed (4)

33

ACROSS

1 Fear landing accident may be the big finish (5,6)
9 Heads down! Toast is here (7,2)
10 Monarch ready to draw the line (5)
11 Congenial address for a ship's captain? (3,3)
12 In very short time the river becomes unsafe (8)
13 Rabies breaks out in the country (6)
15 I'm about to run? Must be an error (8)
18 It's pitiful when dad gets the twitch (8)
19 British sailors occupy a border town in Holland
  – site of World War Two battle (6)
21 Their acts are well-known (8)
23 Unnatural cunning (6)
26 He has skill and courage (5)
27 Anyway, it's where the customs may look (2,3,4)
28 Persuade it's fantasy (4,7)

DOWN

1 Having the hump (7)
2 New cadet deputised (5)
3 Go fishing, but keep in touch (4,1,4)
4 This month in an abbreviated way (4)
5 Writer's addition? It may be taken out in theatre (8)
6 Strange oriental lake (5)
7 Chap concealing a weapon in his clothing (7)
8 Prosper and show off (8)
14 Reasonable desert island with lake (8)
16 Showing a number under the harbour light (9)
17 A short verse on the Shannon river (8)
18 Tells of twinges after exercise (7)
20 Man admitting set up is kind of cross (7)
22 Image to carry to top of mountain (5)
24 Illegally fix games of snooker (5)
25 The French doctor may be frisky (4)

34

ACROSS

1 What international skater won in the polar regions? (6)
5 Built-up urban area? (4,4)
9 To run out, quite upset, for a bandage (10)
10 A bank robber might have it to face (4)
11 Quick witty retort concerning normal starting-place (8)
12 Simple creature in single cell (6)
13 About these days with one Muslim magistrate (4)
15 One may stop playing (8)
18 Train did come off the rails in the West Indies (8)
19 Girl back in North America (4)
21 Found in the Antipodes, S African port (6)
23 Reduce expenditure relating to a deep ditch (8)
25 Spring I pass round (4)
26 Dispiriting (10)
27 Encountered Greek character within, one's making a foul stink (8)
28 One dry concoction over there (6)

DOWN

2 Large number go down – but it was a near thing (5)
3 Flower people getting under the vehicle (9)
4 Unusually thin record brought up to base (6)
5 Home forces (9,6)
6 Allow Henry Gray to move despite the apathy (8)
7 Time to take the strain? (5)
8 Has swab been moved in the bathroom fixture? (9)
14 Mysteriously are moored at the airfield (9)
16 No French individual is a complete nonentity (3-6)
17 A disc-jockey has a little money alongside (8)

20 Awkward when covered with adhesive (6)
22 Airy fairy (5)
24 Stick nothing inside the boat (5)

35

ACROSS

7 Fly without a break, causing stress (8)
9 A group of players quite possibly cross one (6)
10 The likelihood of scraps (4)
11 Part male in composition – it's convention (10)
12 Dull-witted goody-goody taken in by boss (6)
14 Antediluvian enterprise (5,3)
15 Stay on the subject of 9 (6)
17 Institute industrial action and create an impression (6)
20 Military men backing tribal split dealing with dispute (8)
22 Expatriate in a turban is Hindu (6)
23 Topping bread for the aristocracy! (5,5)
24 Many have cut down (4)
25 Chisels back onto firm plaster (6)
26 Lacking capital, and that's no life! (8)

DOWN

1 He's upset 16 – he wants payment (8)
2 A once-respected figure is repeatedly put down (4)
3 The rascally fellow's broken cover, that's clear (6)
4 This neat solution is in doubt (8)
5 Allowance obtained through an embassy (10)
6 On average letters for the queen appear less charitable (6)
8 Go round inflicting injury (6)
13 Coppers taking certain steps in an outbreak (10)
16 The manager of 1 being awkward (8)
18 The Spanish needle one bearing a different way (8)
19 Fail in examinations, and so work as a farm-hand (6)
21 Celebrity taking note about English place (6)
22 Cricketer well-known as a crime-fighter (6)
24 Maidenhead – ancient town (4)

36

ACROSS

1 A French couple needed to relax (7)
5 Dummies found in ruined sofa (4)
9 Government with main traditions for reform (14)
11 Stray cardinal has a condition? (4)
12 Quietly start to pray (5)
13 Ladies' fingers depicted by acceptable artist (4)
16 The heart of the matter (7)
17 Aintree disaster for apprentice (7)
18 Tested the sharpness of sword and pen (4,3)
20 Critical comment – from a theatre critic? (3,4)
22 Many didn't drink after time (4)
23 Note the record is amusing (5)
24 Mushy peas divine to a Scot (4)
27 Hairdressing provided in casualty department (5,9)
28 I reach North Kentucky in the dark (4)
29 Time to think logically about a disloyal act (7)

DOWN

2 Enough to make a hearty editor feel faint? (3,11)
3 A big hit turned back the alliance (4)
4 Stay back with Leslie to have some food (7)
5 A person scorned for striking players? (7)
6 Apprehension felt by Egyptian in remote surroundings (4)
7 Hollow warning from schoolboys after study (7)
8 Nether Wallop (4,2,3,5)
10 He brings a duck back fresh (4)
14 Nothing follows fast for it is very slow (5)
15 In time a theologian may be addressed as father (5)
18 Place for shooting stars? (4,3)
19 Give a graphic description of the harbour light (7)
20 Aggregate and aluminium found in dynamite (7)

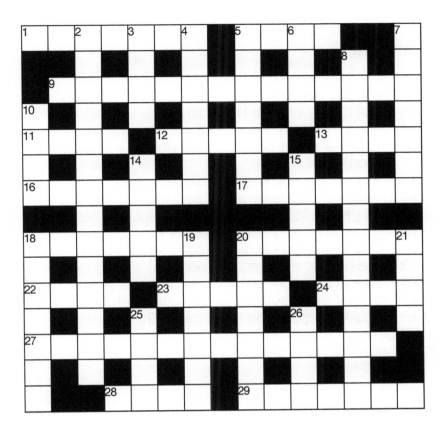

21 Plant of very little note (4)

25 Related some stories in a kindly way (4)

26 See about a thousand duck (4)

37

ACROSS

1 No, I don't aim in any way to gain control (10)
6 Separate section (4)
10 Carol may not catch Henry (5)
11 French money in a South American state (9)
12 "The —— came down like the wolf on the fold" (Byron) (8)
13 Puppy requires women's assistance (5)
15 Listing work done by a cobbler (7)
17 Risk getting left behind the nave (7)
19 A group just likely to succeed (3,4)
21 Civil War battles causing stock-market boom (4,3)
22 Quite right to demand payment (5)
24 Bookkeeper acquires petticoat and suit (4-4)
27 Ensuring that people are well suited (9)
28 Articulate deputy admits nothing (5)
29 Some of the merino sheep need food (4)
30 Under hypnosis English MEP displayed restraint (10)

DOWN

1 Love game (4)
2 Intends to examine benefit claimants (5,4)
3 Trim for a sober gent in New York (5)
4 Causing vexation by combing (7)
5 Set up company to store grain produced naturally (7)
7 Vital for a criminal to be sent back (5)
8 Patrolmen ordered to imprison one bouncer (10)
9 Drink and dance (8)
14 Author describing northern city with style (10)
16 Doing nothing but fighting (8)
18 Can't Irish convert declare his faith? (9)
20 Stay for ceremony incorporating clairvoyance (7)
21 Train bishop to use the phone (5,2)

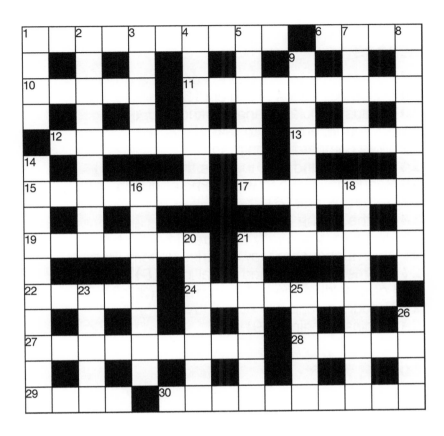

23 Other name for a return voyage (5)
25 The jacket is just about finished (5)
26 Initially taken into consideration, as is fair (4)

38

ACROSS

7 Possess the vocabulary to conduct a quarrel (4,5)
8 Diplomacy keeps one silent (5)
10 Exhaust scholar's range of knowledge (6)
11 Am round, queuing to take drugs (8)
12 More competent workman (6)
14 Most profound look towards the sunset (6)
16 Banner is inscribed with name of queen (4)
17 Get drunk fast (5)
18 Loathe boiling heat (4)
19 Historian is naturally up a tree in Asia (6)
21 As it happens, railway provides uniform (6)
24 Shameless pun timed appallingly (8)
26 Pose, holding medal? If you must! (2,2,2)
27 Announce condition of country (5)
28 Criminal running? (9)

DOWN

1 Stick to prohibit outside (5)
2 Points to case for drug (8)
3 Old officer has an ice-cream (6)
4 A mother? He didn't have one (4)
5 Shout with pain, being inexperienced (6)
6 Mentions a changed 27 (9)
9 Wager about unfortunate accommodation (6)
13 Terrible glare from the king (5)
15 Weakness of one business, Italian, in New York (9)
17 Leatherworker made sixpence once (6)
18 Blue flower unconventional person's taken in to Henry (8)
20 Reward for Bligh's command (6)
22 Gives a funny face (6)
23 Devil runs away from colleague (5)
25 Book, and its author's self-dedication? (4)

39

ACROSS

1 An inch out perhaps, but maintaining contact (2,5)

5 Mention how to rear children (5,2)

9 Window panes need to be placed and fastened (7)

10 Not required for work, a number retire with consent (2,5)

11 Its owner can't be said to have a weak chest! (6-3)

12 In short, Edward is opposed to the current trend, we hear (5)

13 Bear has no right to invest (5)

15 Given a free passage? (9)

17 Bird which is not all crest (9)

19 Goes on the roller-coaster, perhaps (5)

22 Athenian method of working in metal (5)

23 Grow crops – pretty vital, perhaps, inside (9)

25 Offer, or wait for a better offer (4,3)

26 Drink alcohol as a prop (7)

27 Stops in crooked side streets (7)

28 A number baffled and deceived (7)

DOWN

1 I'm old fashioned, there's no getting away from it (7)

2 Rude tot has to be made to be taught (7)

3 A league match (5)

4 Restricted by petty rules, as some in the library (9)

5 Freely born with vote in New York borough (5)

6 Peevishness I shall moderate (3,6)

7 Given protection, being cautious (7)

8 Put on an act in front of nurse (7)

14 Wrong, or sure one is wrong (9)

16 Idle ideas turned out to be made perfect (9)

17 A roof may be tarred (7)

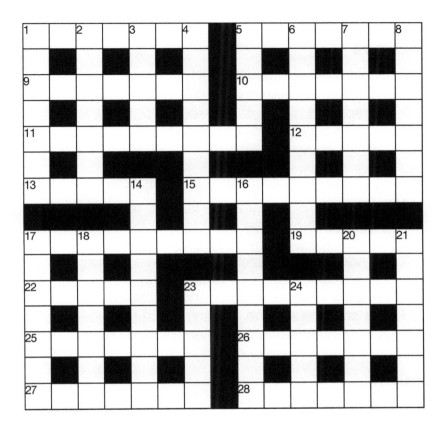

18 Rum soul, perhaps, the brother of Remus (7)
20 Area inside American bases (7)
21 Kind of labour we get fed up about (7)
23 Calls for views to be expressed (5)
24 Drive for mile trip round pithead (5)

40

ACROSS

4 Drunk? Well at a pinch! (5,3)
8 A way with our eagerness (6)
9 Ian replaced bag instantaneously (2,1,5)
10 Groaned about name of hormone (8)
11 Preferably sooner (6)
12 Power of a lawyer? (8)
13 Rover has the frame for a junior officer (8)
16 Old records, only four in the vaulted passages (8)
19 In which one must be quick to get rich? (4-4)
21 Fat goat (6)
23 Not adequately protected, admitted arranging rescue (8)
24 Daughter and I emphasise the trouble (8)
25 Slim engineers of the French church (6)
26 Unfortunately nears end when trapped (8)

DOWN

1 College threesome (7)
2 Not sweetbread from an old-timer! (9)
3 A scrap worn in a Spanish region (6)
4 Not quite recognisable after dieting? (6,9)
5 Lady shortly tatters her best clothes (4,4)
6 It isn't commonly said to be a blemish (5)
7 Batting area near the wicket! (7)
14 Swimmer to prevent copper appearing in drama school (9)
15 Superior speculator to be arrogant (8)
17 Meeting again after a break (7)
18 The one the chorist maltreated is unable to take flight (7)
20 Gleam that could be restful but not loud (6)
22 Giant confetti tangled inside! (5)

41

ACROSS

1 In direct opposition, before guillotine's brought into action? (4-2)
4 Shortage of transport in southern metropolis (8)
9 Cut lumber (6)
10 Winter dancing party? No, but it's thrown for enjoyment (8)
12 Share a role (4)
13 Stuffed dates dished out (5)
14 Originator of intrigue in the past (4)
17 Goat is after vegetable and fruit spread (6,6)
20 Routine arrangements for trippers, perhaps (12)
23 Off on a course (4)
24 When established, something to one's credit (5)
25 Keen to wreck the joint (4)
28 Travel through East End district with offensive weapon (8)
29 Lady bareback rider (6)
30 Move to break concentration (8)
31 Leave behind waste (6)

DOWN

1 It may be played on the lawn in summer (8)
2 Civic dignitary planting tree on isle (8)
3 Alone in Lyon, sadly (4)
5 Supplier of nice cornet? (12)
6 Lines of argument? (4)
7 Prophet is first-class, given a head start (6)
8 Hue and cry at the town centre (6)
11 Clip-joints? (7,5)
15 Should prove uncommonly tough (5)
16 Information about art-form (5)
18 Not a closed range, so start shooting (4,4)
19 Model found to be lacking original parts (8)
21 Managed to get detectives' rank (6)

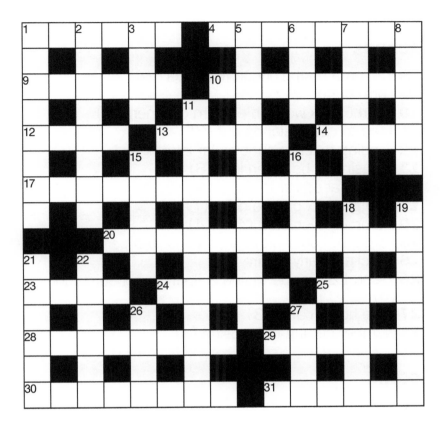

22 As once used in making boats (6)
26 Piece of land is over half a mile (4)
27 Steal note to obtain dress (4)

42

ACROSS

8 Egg on a north London footballer? (4)
9 Farm butter (3)
10 Regret back work on eastern continent (6)
11 Tried to catch Glenda out (6)
12 Tending to leave out circular letter (8)
13 Refusing to be taken in (9,6)
15 Shamefaced cur to be suspended first (7)
17 Wild girl accepts the point (7)
20 Extremely restricted (4,4,3,4)
23 Father at home with bird, a conceited person (8)
25 A jacket nearly on fire (6)
26 Escort Ezra inside to find a Spanish conquistador (6)
27 Take home catch (3)
28 Number batting in Tyneside (4)

DOWN

1 Ask for money to clean up (6)
2 Making it hot for the interviewee (8)
3 Conventional music? (11,4)
4 Take possession of one grand? (7)
5 Number of steps performed reluctantly? (10,5)
6 It will not be used by a certain solver (6)
7 Personalities getting up for a wide boy (4)
14 Daylight (3)
16 Girl almost laid off (3)
18 Left one moggy a vital link (8)
19 Edward, languishing, was going round and round (7)
21 Choice delicacy (6)
22 Repeatedly no zest when it is leaking (6)
24 Nothing is in order in the orchestra (4)

43

ACROSS

1 Erasmus made good use of the rubber (7)
5 Talk when caught by a mad character (7)
9 Remains in vehicle, being wounded (7)
10 Re-classifies places for holidaymakers (7)
11 Inadequate, so tense (9)
12 Come to a stop, the way everybody should do (5)
13 Plant this rose variety after spring's end (5)
15 Feeling for one in time perhaps (9)
17 He'll take issue, finding many over-kind (9)
19 Nick's music (5)
22 Not qualified to speak out (5)
23 Publication for country people – the non-male (9)
25 Rocky English beach (7)
26 Take off a little – trim it at each corner (7)
27 The girl could be slimmer! (7)
28 Most sober and virtuous person after a final home (7)

DOWN

1 Clever people join a top man in hiding (7)
2 A lackadaisical worker made to move smartly (7)
3 Creating sheer chaos in town (5)
4 Made up, having changed (9)
5 The painter must be firm over rubbish (5)
6 Criminals – oafs going around wrong-doing (9)
7 Ground for surrounding the monarch with attendants (7)
8 To break up requires courage (7)
14 Simple optical aid (9)
16 Managed to overturn the salt when telling the tale (9)
17 No clues will be needed by this man of the law (7)
18 Love without object (7)
20 Manipulate work time and a note results! (7)

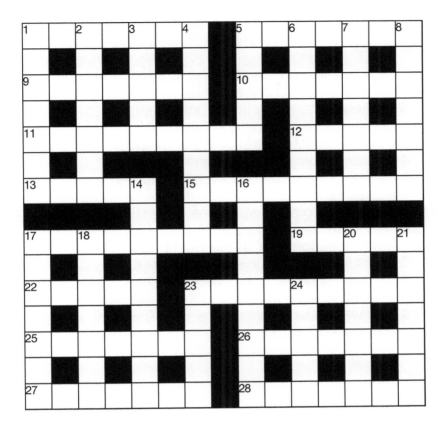

21 Possibly ten tear off to make appeal (7)
23 Cut, but not totally disheartened by it (5)
24 She's caused a large number to leave the USA (5)

44

ACROSS

1 Joint problems of hairiest sort to treat (14)
9 Good states of channels (7)
10 Cricketer with a way in old Holland (7)
11 Comfy home in Gladstone Street (4)
12 Delivery statistics of Erith brats, for example? (10)
14 Extraordinarily manic English films (6)
15 Ugly old figure, she has tweed shortened and altered (8)
17 Large cigar producing flawless ring (8)
18 Sea states required for a jellyfish? (6)
21 Royal seat, formerly, in the High Court (5,5)
22 Elissa, otherwise, achieved nothing (4)
24 Authority showing impropriety (7)
25 Greek character opposed to Italian wine (7)
26 How well do we receive Anne Brontë with a pseudonym? (2,5,2,1,4)

DOWN

1 No cigar is turned out without using chemicals (7)
2 Unsound artistic production of play set in Rome (5,10)
3 More than ancient history, some say (4)
4 Upcountry rugby's given endless credit (6)
5 Hail tuba arrangement as standard (8)
6 Multiply without going forth? (10)
7 Private house? (7,8)
8 Artist with one fault – the grape, that was! (6)
13 Normal pies cooked cold... (10)
16 ...and soon divided, and the like (2,6)
17 The King and I put on in college, but in cramped style (6)
19 Avoiding contact in an informal gathering (7)
20 Bill twice taking first-class return? That is a bloomer! (6)

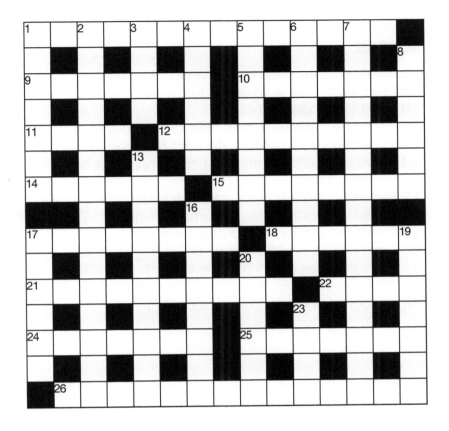

23 Currency bringing Latin air of excitement (4)

45

ACROSS

1 Migratory bird seen by the wharf (10,5)
9 Slaughter a horse in care (7)
10 Guy tries to get fruit (7)
11 Provide a labourer temporarily to help out (4,1,4)
12 In Europe radio broadcasts work of note (5)
13 Make insensitive daughter accept hopeless situation (4,3)
15 Cautious about it being seen as philanthropy (7)
17 Somehow obtain a large number of plants (7)
19 Clearly stated by former newsmen (7)
21 Course a drunkard imbibes champagne initially! (5)
23 Unusually fierce sea battle ends with it (5-4)
25 Where etymologists may find interest briefly (2,1,4)
26 Portent of an era before wisdom? (7)
27 Go to bed, duck (3,4,4,4)

DOWN

1 Gratified by having caught a trout (7)
2 A king and queen on an island off Scotland (5)
3 Alien male shattered by 8th-Army victory (2,7)
4 Lure fish back from the sheltered side (7)
5 Unsettled by cross depicted in crude icon (7)
6 Is allowed to produce a piece of poetry (5)
7 All together formerly (2,3,4)
8 Yes, cats can provide great delight (7)
14 Greek seaman displaying dry humour (5,4)
16 Dread having to make an arrest (9)
17 Giving support is refreshing (7)
18 Chirpy little creatures (7)
19 Model is no longer well-proportioned (7)
20 Has herself visited the liquor house? (7)
22 Prickly old English character (5)
24 It metamorphosed one minute previously (5)

46

ACROSS

1 Italian food is the finished article (5)
4 But he helps out the rest of the week too (3,6)
9 Lieutenant covered by complete protection (7)
11 Relief from soldiers' malice (7)
12 Keep left in brick-transporter (4)
13 Jack or King East received – not this card though? (5)
14 Girl is to finish about one (4)
17 Boss's assistant, commonly a girl, an African high-flier (9,4)
19 Characters from Magdalen scorn such a gossip (13)
21 Family keeps money in tin (4)
22 Seize a point, making a complaint (5)
23 Pub is to north of farm building (4)
26 Tablet one takes on passenger seat (7)
27 Rest leg, damaged in race (2,5)
28 Possible harm, going round different Yorkshire town (9)
29 Subdued, we tucked into fish (5)

DOWN

1 How fast we run to pillar-box? (9)
2 Woman will overlook bill for varnish (7)
3 Opposed to contents of Asian Times (4)
5 Child's room is not even somewhere to learn in the winter (7,6)
6 Flower came up (4)
7 Stooped to dig – need straightening (7)
8 Make submission for grant (5)
10 Thoroughly associating cause with development (4,3,6)
15 There's nothing of the animal in him (5)
16 Guide I brought in to conspiracy (5)

18 Poor road, so ran from the plant (6,3)
19 Red clarets drunk (7)
20 City's light interrupted by gas explosion (7)
21 Skip to take exercise in vehicle (5)
24 A substitute for sin (4)
25 Almost obstruct united group of countries (4)

47

ACROSS

1 Incorrect kit means trouble (8)
6 Pub arranged to have meals in every bar (6)
9 Demon drink? (6)
10 Tides ebb about workers seeking alluvial deposit (8)
11 Sole assistance for those travelling in the Arctic (8)
12 Possibly secure and free from danger (6)
13 What an MP stands for (12)
16 It cannot safely be ignored (6,6)
19 Why brides may conceal having mixed parentage (6)
21 His paper turned to stone (8)
23 After which the participants come out of their shells (4,4)
24 Famous London columnist (6)
25 Maintain there's some body in the beer (6)
26 He won the race, we hear by a hair's breadth? (8)

DOWN

2 Threaten one politician with death (6)
3 Projected through sound (5)
4 General stew thickener (9)
5 Beginning the Northern climb (7)
6 Not above using two foreign articles (5)
7 Take offensive action in two ways, producing great surprise (9)
8 Make it known the girl's gained little weight (8)
13 It may be tipped but not recommended by doctors (9)
14 Metal key used by the cook (3,6)
15 Childlike woman's body writhing in the dance (4,4)
17 Vet gets bug out of parrot's head (7)

18 Wrongs, a source of Shakespearian comedy (6)
20 Sailor died a dissolute man (5)
22 He will shortly ring – for your reply (5)

48

ACROSS

1 Bill's presented (7,8)
9 Rush herb out and put in another bed (9)
10 A young lady is wrong (5)
11 Lubricates with ink splashed on waterproof (7)
12 A little fine weather for the festival (7)
13 Italian leader engineers rage (3)
14 Rudi, struggling in Dick's endless embrace, is concerned with ancient Celts (7)
17 Lose hope of the French couple (7)
19 It has some pull when the following vehicle has no power (7)
22 Urge along to fashionable type of cinema (5-2)
24 Born to one expecting inside (3)
25 Left out order, Edward held it (7)
26 European bridge, his construction (7)
28 Resident physician endlessly offers cover (5)
29 Flying expenses? (9)
30 Blown away? That's novel (4,4,3,4)

DOWN

1 It gives a better atmosphere indoors (3-12)
2 Penny, amongst black fuel, found some hard resin (5)
3 Girl removing desk had not been invited (7)
4 It, in crazy antic, was huge (7)
5 Provided with a permanent income now deed has matured (7)
6 Publications in which the days are numbered (7)
7 Control, say, to being back to its former position (9)
8 Not able to choose between one party or another? (15)
15 Laws that can't be removed from the statute-book (9)
16 Simple content little devil (3)

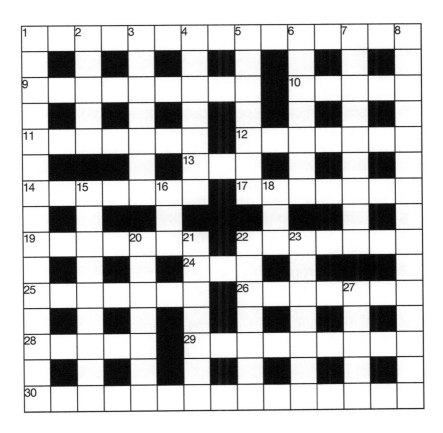

18 Sin of eastern bishop (3)
20 How one might get too big for one's boots? (7)
21 Finish with the majority farthest away (7)
22 Not going up this slope? (7)
23 Man to do some gardening – that's novel (7)
27 Terrorists question first person, a Middle Easterner (5)

49

ACROSS

7 Sacked a representative exposing miners to danger (8)
9 Construction of doe pen must be started (6)
10 Having a credit note, gives ground (4)
11 One's pride's being damaged. Can result in low spirits (10)
12 Equip in flexible fashion (6)
14 Devotee of a single party after a while (8)
15 A painter getting the wind up? (6)
17 Making such a suit a man needs expertise (6)
20 Journalist writing about ale (8)
22 The French turn on the water (6)
23 Deal fairly with a colleague in a sensible way (10)
24 Many take off, that's the point (4)
25 A young lady scoffed, causing dispute (6)
26 Builders in secret or otherwise (8)

DOWN

1 Overlook the markdown (8)
2 Sound seed yield (4)
3 Scarcely daring to accept money (6)
4 Remonstrance for having duplicated invitation (4,4)
5 A ringer-up's quite possibly floored! (7,3)
6 Put down RAF officers in a letter (6)
8 Calls – finds Father's at home (4,2)
13 Police raid may be made from time to time (10)
16 No longer cared for, being so lengthy (8)
18 They'll purchase a jumper on board (8)
19 Bars giving the old king Continental articles (6)
21 He avoids backing the revolutionary way (6)
22 Meanly treated non-professionals (6)
24 Allude to it in church (4)

50

ACROSS

1 Suspicious, if retiring and bashful (5)
4 Leap with spirit in square-dancing for kids (9)
8 Prepared to learn unknown amount (5)
9 Are pub hours recorded in it? (5,4)
11 Carry on with payment for services (4)
12 Wielding guns I turn (5)
13 Seabirds return with another variety (4)
16 Trendy valet in trouble by accident (13)
19 Reading between the lines, normally (8,5)
20 Star part chosen by Bassanio (4)
22 Circumference right after treatment? (5)
23 Inclination to be crooked (4)
26 Prepared tongue that makes one repast (9)
27 Dominion's true majesty (5)
28 Secret USA invention they cut back... (9)
29 ...Washington with range of knowledge to stimulate? (5)

DOWN

1 Handel wrote music for them in a burst of temper (9)
2 Hilton country in which girl has an accident (7-2)
3 Twice, you fail to finish this plaything (2-2)
4 Alf, for example, showing old gold piece? (4-9)
5 Feeling the chill, being one hundred years of age (4)
6 Judge of delicate Mozart piece? (5)
7 He, given any break, will be laughing (5)
10 Agnostic? Goner, mixing in these groups! (13)
14 Novelist in fine fettle (5)
15 Dandies of British and French waters (5)
17 Only one subject in this leisure area? (5,4)
18 Many chats about Chichester, for example (9)
20 City guides announced (5)

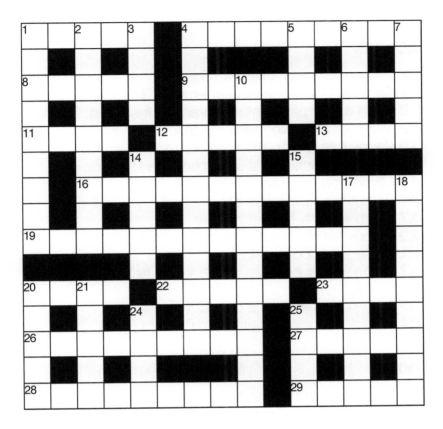

21 Jelly eaten with a relish, mostly (5)
24 Greek and Italian resolution (4)
25 Mark out in a tie (4)

51

ACROSS

1 Assemble to do a jigsaw (5,8)
7 Go to work despite disagreement (3,2)
8 Bring round payment in advance? Just joking! (9)
9 Meet for a session with the tailor (7)
10 Penny has a plan to complete (4,3)
11 Portrait in Gericault's style contains little colour (5)
12 Missed tea brewed up in a cup (9)
14 Versatile fellow takes team into the yard (4-5)
17 Informed of a type of pottery (5)
19 Where hospital visitors went shortly before? (7)
21 Not a good-looker (4,3)
22 Ambassador needs preparation to get capital cover (4-5)
23 American objective is correct (5)
24 Stimulant for malodorous old sailors (8,5)

DOWN

1 Get attired in the garment and pose (3,2,2)
2 Key reason for arousing passion (7)
3 Have to get out of bed – admit it (3,2)
4 The Spanish agent resolved to be stylish (7)
5 Abominable man, and one with intelligence (7)
6 Tory design never accepted by Socialist bishop (5,8)
7 Strikers need to have secure marriages (6,7)
8 Claim hard-headed parent has capital (7)
13 "Why, this is very midsummer —— ."
Shakespeare's *Twelfth Night* (7)
15 Modern entrance to old prison (7)
16 The way uneducated apprentice made pastry (7)
17 A large article I left for the maid (7)
18 Eternal appeal of *Peter Pan*? (7)
20 Rigorous manoeuvres set by the navy (5)

52

ACROSS

1 Bird – see head emerge from shell (8)
5 Chat with criminal is really great (6)
9 Refuse to travel in such a vehicle (8)
10 Whoops! Sleeve got dipped in river (4,2)
12 Slightly mad person in Genoa (9)
13 Quick writer of satires (5)
14 Flip one's lid? (4)
16 To catch trout, enter the right little stream (7)
19 A match for Satan (7)
21 Proverbially smooth lawyer (4)
24 Lament doctor going to pot (5)
25 Important party needs second butler (5-4)
27 Newspaper in convulsion – very sad (6)
28 Is very bad at playing Schubert arrangement (8)
29 Tea so spoiled, but drunk (6)
30 Commit offence, performing at Edinburgh? (8)

DOWN

1 A number remove clothes and go to sleep (3,3)
2 It's Susan's handkerchief (6)
3 Royal meeting a Northerner (5)
4 Metro station? (3-4)
6 Ills prove devastating for displaced population (9)
7 Why people play football – to have excitement (3,5)
8 Article found in loaf, it is whispered (8)
11 Band has a hit (4)
15 Faint line redrawn, being undeveloped (9)
17 Plant list came out (8)
18 Correct bill given to clergyman (8)
20 Frost's verse is heard (4)
21 Stay a day in France, housed by relative (7)
22 Hurry up and make progress (4,2)
23 Mickey, say, eats second sweet (6)
26 Happen again to need some more currency (5)

53

ACROSS

1 Avoid showing fright when catching the ball (7)
5 To succeed, it must follow her in first (7)
9 Largely in royal fashion (7)
10 A sitter becoming a performer (7)
11 Give two pounds, nothing more, for an old master (9)
12 Marks or pounds? (5)
13 Sound director made fun of (5)
15 Make sure as sure can be (9)
17 Existing fashion? (4,5)
19 State of birth (5)
22 The one to right of them (5)
23 Accept a holiday and say goodbye (4,5)
25 Football official on the application form? (7)
26 In mental disorder I suffer from it (7)
27 Holder of the colours (7)
28 Pardons and releases (7)

DOWN

1 Light shadow on the log hearth (7)
2 English period showing unusual energy about the first century (7)
3 Spectacular effect when powder magazine finally goes up (5)
4 Two blues for British hearties (5,4)
5 State aid distributed by the Home Office (5)
6 For such an accident, call bronzed doctor, one from overseas (3-3-3)
7 The stone archaeologists treat so cryptically (7)
8 After the start of trial, argue the cause of a crime (7)
14 Run away twice? Not this soldier! (6,3)
16 Restrain a friend in final defeat (9)
17 Allows to rest peacefully? Quite the opposite! (4,3)

18 Upset rum truffle (7)
20 Red Star delivery for dealers (7)
21 *Lear* production set up with part of *Hamlet* (7)
23 Subject he met in form (5)
24 Shrub I ring up about (5)

54

ACROSS

7 & 8 Sailor on land among the choice few? (4,2,3,5)

10 Mat has aggravated respiratory disorder (6)

11 Do work on hand (8)

12 Mowed a ploughed field (6)

14 In the alcove, let Alice take a few steps (6)

16 Document does not quite correspond (4)

17 Idiot accepted model had progressed (3,2)

18 Who's going out to demonstrate? (4)

19 Thousand in tale that's turbulent (6)

21 Deviating but finding another way in Grangemouth (6)

24 One can do tricks with a snake (8)

26 Bony runner to the north of New York (6)

27 & 28 Higher then they moved the ruler (5,3,6)

DOWN

1 & 15 Not real semblances of deception (5,9)

2 Most irritating or most catty, but not to start with (8)

3 Frightened by a strong attack (6)

4 Has moved first bit of meat paste (4)

5 What's in it may not be discovered until the present time (6)

6 & 23 Very quickly in the main (2,1,4,2,5)

9 Ragged one in Rouen with senior churchman (6)

13 For what reason is it included on the tree? (5)

15 See 1

17 Man with article on a South American country (6)

18 Got in as a stranger in the city (8)

20 Disc broken at athletics (6)

22 Cleaner part of a tap? (6)

23 See 6

25 One outside hospital might need treatment for this (4)

55

ACROSS

1 A tale concocted by Oriental eccentric (8)
5 Small vehicle rating as a divine thing once (6)
9 "The wild —— leaps in glory." Tennyson's *The Princess* (8)
10 Foolish people left without a word of thanks (6)
11 Plastered, so gave up (8)
12 Gets down to work in an ocean-going vessel (6)
14 For a Tory it's an anomaly still (10)
18 The main issue well presented at a suitable time (10)
22 Jewish ambassador needing a drink (6)
23 A ship in which sherry is often served (8)
24 The person who's called on to deal with complaints (6)
25 Playing – but not playing fair (8)
26 Yearned for golden make-up (6)
27 Tear around endlessly showing respect (8)

DOWN

1 Put down superior performance (6)
2 When overdue, a lot of books may be hidden (6)
3 The painter might appear a twister (6)
4 Bands for controlling wayward cart-horses (10)
6 Given credit, scoff – no-one backs the concept (8)
7 An allowance not quite everybody finds reasonable (8)
8 The highest scorer being really sweet (5,3)
13 A stony dependant (10)
15 This bloomer had Poles bewildered (8)
16 In London, with a swift horse, one can make it! (8)
17 A green vegetable sustained the merry old soul (8)
19 Pasta or pate? (6)
20 Draw some apprentices at work (6)
21 There's contention about the right alarm (6)

56

ACROSS

1 Spy a refined sort of chap? (5)
4 Four-letter word that upsets Margaret T (9)
8 Cockney's comic artist is at Covent Garden (5)
9 Ropy way of letting oneself down (9)
11 Has a little Greek (4)
12 Up and about in a shake (5)
13 Air of boy starting geometry (4)
16 Non-racial game, perhaps, of transatlantic relations? (5-8)
19 What doctors say can not be passed on, touchingly (3-10)
20 River trial (4)
22 Precocious little girl who could go either way? (5)
23 House found in home counties, by motorway (4)
26 As score came up, it went the wrong way (9)
27 Stays, the highest on board? (5)
28 Fan of former farm-vehicle (9)
29 Grounds, for example, held by doctors (5)

DOWN

1 Get into a boil about ban (9)
2 Watches locomotive that has trouble with lamps (9)
3 Knock back some of the gin (4)
4 New tan carpets for restaurant, by the way (9,4)
5 A boundary put up in league (4)
6 Old money one charges in Africa (5)
7 Giant figure makes Mum curious (5)
10 One keeps records of ground-rents (13)
14 Gleaming silver brassed off? (5)
15 Lower half of dining-room for curry (5)
17 Cereals so wrong in a covered oven-dish (9)
18 He believed he was winning on the pools (9)
20 It must be turned over on the tenth (5)

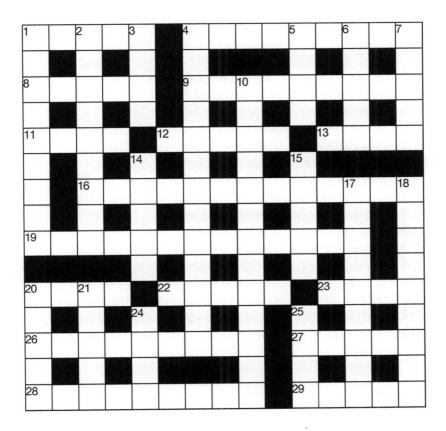

21 Fish used to stink (5)
24 Mount wrapped in blanket, Naturally (4)
25 Employed editor to support you and me? (4)

57

ACROSS

1 His fare is nevertheless expensive in France (7)
5 Let none of the debt be paid (7)
9 A pound note initially made very small (7)
10 Encounter causes argument to follow (3,4)
11 Army supporter served with a drink (5)
12 Find out about sectarian differences (9)
13 Prohibition keeping Sandhurst inactive (7)
14 Nurse grabs top-class trainee by the rump (4-3)
16 Contract to construct a viaduct (7)
19 Rex strolled and strolled (7)
22 Airman left despite being found innocent (9)
24 Irish leader embraced by Scandinavian woman (5)
25 Lively article I meant to get circulated (7)
26 Embarrassed a lady in poor accommodation (7)
27 For that reason he came in to negotiate (7)
28 Pressman in pursuit of drug went hell for leather (7)

DOWN

1 Meditate in bed if bewildered (7)
2 Mediterranean port is fuller-flavoured (7)
3 Dog Dad's Army? (4,5)
4 I learnt to become trusting (7)
5 After a month it contains firm fruit (7)
6 Many a remarkable man is solitary (5)
7 RAF unit dined with Chindit chief (7)
8 Physician admitted being inundated (7)
15 I am to act as arbiter next (9)
16 The first male worker to be really resolute (7)
17 Need about 25 sheets (7)
18 Some rotten treatment suffered by those who beg (7)
19 MP makes Labourites accept EU farming policy (7)

20 Bound to find female in the van (7)
21 Recoiled from adder disturbed by Edward (7)
23 One judge is in a temper (5)

58

ACROSS

1 Remarkably neat, trim disciplinarian (8)
6 Laid back about sergeant major causing depression (6)
9 Stays determined to pursue the French horn (6)
10 Return enthusiasm (8)
11 Protective clothing commanded by Corcoran (8)
12 A painter has returned from the desert (6)
13 The finest area to be a National Park (4,8)
16 Day before the present day? (9,3)
19 Agree to study dog (6)
21 Pass mark? (8)
23 Suspicion that damp leads to corrosion (8)
24 Parade-ground command is a joke (2,4)
25 Wrote in prison? (6)
26 Sort of ring for a long time (8)

DOWN

2 A Spaniard is a handsome man (6)
3 In panto, scant role for opera singer (5)
4 Hang on less tightly (3,2,4)
5 Incline to be unwell internally – it's the back (4-3)
6 Takes out some fruit (5)
7 Extra burden for fish caught in swell (9)
8 Purloin a modern painting (8)
13 Royal person not up at university (9)
14 New town still in process of development (9)
15 Form view the hill has nothing inside (8)
17 A job given to the French missionary (7)
18 I'd best move living quarters (3-3)
20 Serving of sandwiches – not this shape surely? (5)
22 Hard back (5)

59

ACROSS

1 An outstanding part of the country (8)
9 How a bright idea comes to you? (2,1,5)
10 Cattle complaint (4)
11 Provides what was necessary and completes the account (5,3,4)
13 A spot of sympathy? (8)
15 Soldier who had a point in joining the army (6)
16 Low average (4)
17 Rita's out of step (5)
18 Observed and heard making a scene (4)
20 Duke Ellington's mood? (6)
21 Elegant braid one makes (8)
23 Etiquette observed by the board (5,7)
26 They have a strong pull in the port trade (4)
27 Apt to be not on the level (8)
28 Perhaps Ned does right to get confirmed (8)

DOWN

2 Watch part required for a telescope? (3-5)
3 The gear demanded by skilled workers? (12)
4 Branch of the deer family (6)
5 Appreciates one's accommodation (4)
6 Composer has part written up for a single man (8)
7 Jump bail in Asian isle (4)
8 The issue of marriage? (8)
12 Bred in sin, set out this indication of it? (4,8)
14 Spent about a pound for cloth (5)
16 Claim support (8)
17 Row not unexpected in Ulster's parliament (8)
19 Close of play (8)
22 Made tea for the family, say (6)
24 Start with a dollar? (4)
25 Artist's model who barely earns a living? (4)

60

ACROSS

1 Restrain explorer losing weight (7)
5 Until 'e's disposed of the household vessel (7)
9 Marooned sailor with a single old penny (9)
10 Woman in gold fancy hat outside (5)
11 Small South African laboratory destroyed wood (5)
12 Set aside when it had been identified (9)
13 Unknowns see telephone instrument gets tapped (9)
16 This has a disheartening effect on apples, for example (5)
17 More accurate, that's more typical (5)
18 Paint verses about the other side of the world (9)
20 It's a long diversion, having a sentimental longing for the past (9)
23 In the south of France returning to the river (5)
25 Fruit from Antigua vandalised (5)
26 Delay rate increase (9)
27 Replaced the soap at the café (7)
28 Got into a twist when model did some fishing (7)

DOWN

1 Takes a stand on case, so to speak (7)
2 Make use of protection for the face, we hear (5)
3 He snatches the little goat while asleep (9)
4 Man has Irene's make-up (5)
5 Not above having examined what is next to the floorboards (9)
6 Get more out of modern art? (5)
7 Thwarted on board perhaps (9)
8 Greek name in editorial (7)
14 State "Girl hugs boy" (9)
15 Butterfly fruit? Mine's over! (6-3)
16 Tropical sign? (9)
17 The approaching darkness (7)

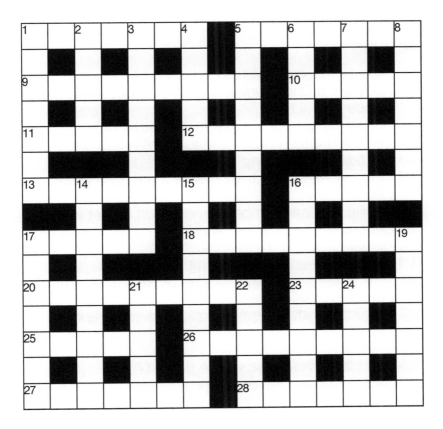

19 Stop payment – we object during pay out (7)
21 Covered an area of the North Sea (5)
22 Let Frenchman into the passage (5)
24 Go right through the exercise (5)

61

ACROSS

1 Transfer directors at the exchange (11)
8 Not even a Chopin lover objects to miscellaneous pieces (4,3,4)
11 Still, it might be a subject for the artist (4)
12 Comes in a tea-chest individually (4)
13 Got fed up with being derided (7)
15 Get dunderhead to twist before the French weaken (7)
16 Got up in a bad temper – is enraged in fact (5)
17 Set-backs do not affect Auntie (4)
18 Dispute backing it – very loudly (4)
19 Sounds like unprepossessing fruit (5)
21 Turn to greeting one of Shakespeare's characters (7)
22 Instructor finds a beverage expensive in France (7)
23 Cheese made anew (4)
26 Don't leave a film sequence uncut (4)
27 Sacking in old Chester outpost (11)
28 Making public announcements diverting as can be (11)

DOWN

2 Ford put certain points about publicity (4)
3 More appetising variety artiste (7)
4 Cards for a worker (4)
5 A wall with only nine green bottles? Not in this puzzle! (3,4)
6 The last thing one might be taken for (4)
7 The puffer from Waterford? (5,6)
8 Like a mad dog, and an Englishman's topee in the midday sun (3,4,4)
9 A snack for the cannibal? (8,3)
10 Timid stockholder with wide-ranging interests (5,6)

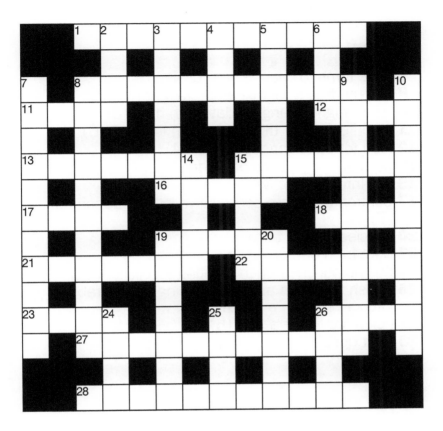

14 Dog in a stew (5)

15 Entry on the left made by one in arrears (5)

19 Howl when girl gets up to stir tea (7)

20 Not all will be pleased a testy fellow calms down (7)

24 Crazy about energy-packed drink (4)

25 Being in good taste, they may well let it stand (4)

26 Unable to decide if it has been damaged (4)

62

ACROSS

7 Take turns to change neat design (9)
8 It is not true a moral can be taught by it (5)
10 Rose might arrange a date with men (8)
11 A conference of tribesmen from Ibadan? (6)
12 Idea for softening top of flan (4)
13 Outstanding feature of Cinders' sisters (8)
15 Got into very hot water (7)
17 Confronted by two consecutive letters rubbed out (7)
20 Fancies current account charges (8)
22 Sore from damaging London statue (4)
25 Pull no punches when greeting a solicitor (3,3)
26 Jewish teacher's attempt at being an incurably inferior player in a game (8)
27 Poles are to set a trap (5)
28 Aunt upset, worn out, ready for a bath (9)

DOWN

1 Franciscan mission not entirely fashionable (5)
2 Herb Hutton returned to the marsh (6)
3 An insect mutation for example (8)
4 Arrangement to admit us into the sports-ground (7)
5 Flower produced despite poor drainage (8)
6 Fine sculpturing material results from a laboratory bloomer (9)
9 Thrilling, nothing; just a little flower (4)
14 Provides opportunities (9)
16 It was left to sailors in the old days (8)
18 Small mark left by bloodsucker is only a trifle (4-4)
19 Female Russian artisan in trouble (7)
21 Roman statesman, one interested in jazz-circle? (4)
23 Start, or I'll take an alcoholic drink (6)
24 Enter unusual items in an auction, maybe (5)

63

ACROSS

1 Drink dropped at critical juncture (9)
9 The tragic lover who grew a beard about 50 (7)
10 The character of a bore (7)
11 Storage place for bread and wine (3)
12 Impair butter that is turned over (3)
13 Water for a mother pig (5,4)
15 Curious people on back street causing scraps (8)
16 Make a man of, say? (6)
18 Put a stop to six-footer? That's very hard! (7)
21 Make effervescent return after a disastrous tea (6)
24 Tennis ie played by a Nobel prizewinner (8)
26 Twisted coils after a time vibrate (9)
27 Cop backs prohibition (3)
28 Setback for the German or Communist? (3)
29 Pen love-letters, perhaps, and wrap them up (7)
30 The horse carrying a large figure appeared hot (7)
31 Hear I'd go after two under par with 20/20 vision (5-4)

DOWN

2 The devil is a most evil fellow (7)
3 Puzzles formulated in games (7)
4 Bob made childish progress at writing? (8)
5 Lay-priest accommodated by theologian practised sponging (6)
6 Airmen ate in mess to refresh the body (2-7)
7 Playing jazz and interfering with reception (7)
8 One receiving a letter about what to wear (9)
14 The usual answer given by the French (7)
16 Enthusiasm is shown as new gear's seen (9)
17 It will signal Doomsday for desperate card player (4,5)
19 Grand event, of course (8)

20 Made it possible for Eugenia to get a phlebotomy (7)

22 Mrs Ruff left one inside to give solace (7)

23 Valve used to deter vandalism (7)

25 Do I die digesting poisonous salt? (6)

64

ACROSS

1 Area of Ireland in which real kid is processed (7)
5 An Italian writer of music played rather slowly (7)
9 Was successful as a croupier (5,2,3,5)
10 Fixture not found at home (4)
11 Detest coming from harbour leaving ancient city behind (5)
12 One who is not in favour ain't troubled (4)
15 Seek loo out for inspection (4-3)
16 Resentment at counterfeit gone astray (7)
17 Fail to get experience when the young lady is 10 (4,3)
19 Finished everywhere (3,4)
21 Not applicable, provided it is artless (4)
22 Couple getting support (5)
23 Small bolt NB is replaced (4)
26 The usual habit of a doctor? (7,8)
27 In the corridor, man there who is not very active (7)
28 Accommodation for Mr Lawrence at French town (7)

DOWN

1 Cur, say, with Sarah going round a reception room at the spa (7)
2 Similar to meaty chunks perhaps, dressed up (4,1,4,6)
3 Useful cockney fellow (4)
4 Give a subject a title perhaps (7)
5 Mad dash for a place in Kent (7)
6 Empty out onto the rubbish heap (4)
7 Keeping out of trouble? That's the policy (3-12)
8 Delightful city is an absurdity (7)
13 A tax popular with race-goers! (5)
14 Unevenly? (5)
17 Ran the way the director did? (7)

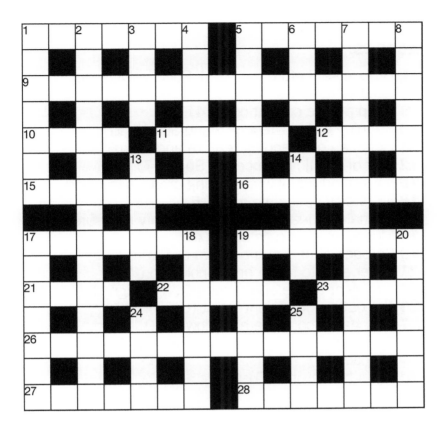

18 It was permitted after biting small pie (7)
19 Doomed dogs trapped by wild cat going round (7)
20 In which things are taken the wrong way (7)
24 Dry up after a song (4)
25 Form of worship I pore over (4)

65

ACROSS

1 Grub is set before the head. Such indulgence! (10)
9 Keep an eye on soft ooze (4)
10 Running water – test of manufacture (10)
11 Finish an outstanding feature and win (6)
12 Sort of elastic produced in Spain (7)
15 A wary individual where giving credit is involved (7)
16 Agitatedly paces the room (5)
17 Animals in quarantine – a temporary measure (4)
18 Money left by single artist (4)
19 Setback after a number turn awkward (3,2)
21 Never able to reach any conclusion (7)
22 A story or article about being in a foreign city (7)
24 The outlaw of ancient Egypt (6)
27 Infer game could be a let-down (10)
28 Rating about dunderhead repeatedly given chances (4)
29 Thought of twin (10)

DOWN

2 Calling for a little sweet-natured mount (4)
3 Most sound and sober person without regrets (6)
4 Makes essential points about Latin translation (7)
5 To be uppity is certainly not a good thing (4)
6 Still considering including the French (7)
7 Mundane use of net praised extravagantly (10)
8 Give thanks for increase (10)
12 Gathering there's nothing way-out (10)
13 A dray tends to break down so be prepared (5,5)
14 Greek character taken in by the City's legendary tales (5)
15 Frisky cur, and so clean! (5)
19 Going to pieces, like junior (7)

20 East European holding the club up could be drunk (7)

23 A large number break loose (6)

25 Youngster showing a bit of leg (4)

26 "X" is after silver, so money-changing (4)

66

ACROSS

1 Perturb the workers, but conclude a deal (5,5)
6 Pert female comes with insolence (4)
10 Seat one gets into daily (5)
11 French wine enters USA to be drunk (9)
12 Submitted to the Spanish Guard (8)
13 Magic spell is about to do damage (5)
15 Admit objective is a bad mistake (3,4)
17 Enticingly shows daughter to old tribesmen (7)
19 Always going express (3-4)
21 Whip firm into sudden spurt (7)
22 The snow-line? (5)
24 No special item selected from many thin garments (8)
27 As a professional he may be painfully manipulative (9)
28 Pronounce complete (5)
29 Loophole in strong regulation (4)
30 Lack of generosity gave sharp pain to one head (10)

DOWN

1 Big bag of plunder (4)
2 Among men, a remarkable Greek leader (9)
3 Regret having taken head off bird (5)
4 Club found in weapon store (7)
5 Ran and just made the five ten (7)
7 Notice nothing's turned up for her (5)
8 New stamps sure to receive approval (4,6)
9 Beautiful singing could be noble act (3,5)
14 Good demonstration of being impervious to noise? (10)
16 How to take a kangaroo unawares? (2,3,3)
18 Handled glasses (9)

20 Take part in show, having informal agreement to include amateur (4-3)

21 Tell me how much you need for a drink (3,4)

23 Starts to see urgent truths, reading an Eastern scripture (5)

25 A certain time with one voluptuous charmer (5)

26 Girl keeping pupil in (4)

67

ACROSS

1 It's right to give some sort of a smile (7)
5 Struggle with large discrepancy – about 2p (7)
9 Produced from hot coals if the girl stirs them up (9)
10 A very low joint (5)
11 20 might grow fatter (7)
12 Eighth month had exciting start for circus clown (7)
13 Think about what a shoplifter does? (4,5)
16 The wine got left inside – very remiss (5)
17 Two notes to the Roman leader about the sun (5)
18 Measuring against the average in future (9)
21 Right to take a bit back from a ticket showing he's paid (7)
22 Hurried back at speed to tell the story (7)
25 Caught in bungled CIA plants (5)
26 A race involving one thousand can nevertheless, be very lively (9)
27 Moans about a pound and a quarter spent on present day vehicles (7)
28 Retsina which has gone off is not so nice! (7)

DOWN

1 Umpire allowed 100 in to meditate (7)
2 Trouble about extremes of power in the Spring (5)
3 Executing a murderer makes one feel less well (5)
4 It attracted nothing but a small generator (7)
5 Move away from the situation to find something that was missing (3,4)
6 First class lasagne can stop the pain (9)
7 Asian makes up the paint I ask for (9)
8 Horse condition was the last of these on which we used spoon (3-4)
14 King I see on a bike with frequency (9)

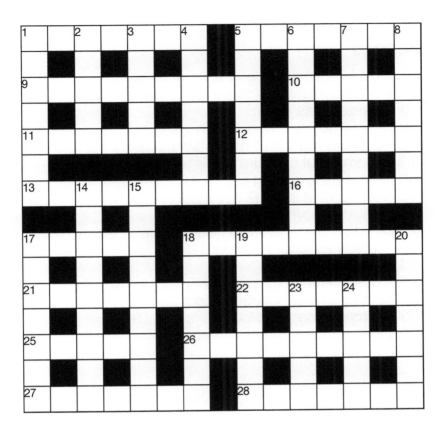

15 Forcing Carol to take public transport (9)

17 Tidies up the trees (7)

18 Coppers taking in sailor raising a weapon (7)

19 Chap going to Jerusalem has a very nice house (7)

20 One who picks up what's left from 11 (7)

23 Nothing in computer memories moves without a reason (5)

24 A Liberal I excuse (5)

68

ACROSS

1 Provides camouflage of animal skins (5)
4 Wartime volunteers made rough preparations (4,5)
8 Secretary has no time (5)
9 Agent who must keep within limits? (2-7)
11 Plague in Hamelin? That's awful (4)
12 Supernatural creature that's after information (5)
13 A guy has to wait (4)
16 Keep turning in bed? Not at all (5,4,1,3)
19 What dear loves murmur? (5,8)
20 Question persistently to give backup to redcap (4)
22 Irritation as lapdog is heard (5)
23 It's just light (4)
26 A talk in French for confidentiality (4-1-4)
27 Nothing pleasant gets postponed (2,3)
28 Wretched chap, to blockade a port (9)
29 Went out about noon and ate (5)

DOWN

1 Casual greeting to the right girl (3-2-4)
2 Coffee set is made badly (9)
3 In winter, it's the making of a man (4)
4 His Excellency contracted to expand into munitions (4,9)
5 Old tribesman contributed to killing others (4)
6 Hesitation in a junior officer's warning (5)
7 Man obsessed with his appearance is comic (5)
10 Brummie is shut out of London tourist attraction (7,6)
14 Priest didn't finish page of book (5)
15 Girl was an ass (5)
17 Islander could be such a devil (9)
18 One has corresponding appeal (3,6)
20 Apostle is safe (5)
21 Satisfied about *Old Testament* anthem (5)

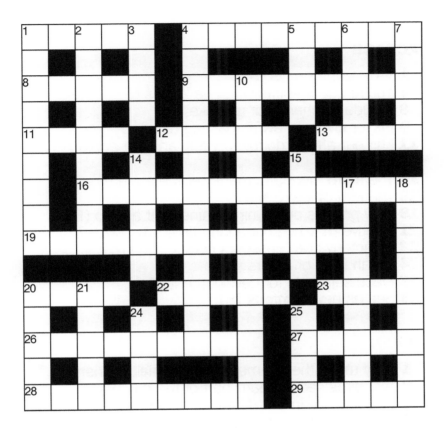

24 Fabric of the French church (4)
25 Dismissed, we hear, for being cheeky (4)

69

ACROSS

1 VAT, say, for nails (5)
4 You're out of spirits when he leaves (8)
8 Intrude by chance or mistake (8)
9 Player given an awful roasting (8)
11 I hit out after a double century and get applause (7)
13 The more there are, the fewer there are (9)
15 The Met office (3,8,4)
18 New proof is put to ninety-nine, half asleep (9)
21 Captive may be shot a long time afterwards (7)
22 Monotony of a Massenet composition (8)
24 Italian man of affairs (8)
25 Place set aside for development (4,4)
26 See as new comforts (5)

DOWN

1 They make their names as proverbial listeners (3,7)
2 Two birds seen in early part of the day (8)
3 Picadors are involved here and there (8)
4 Repeat after some reflection (4)
5 Stay to check mother in (6)
6 Encourage a sound location for a pub (6)
7 Yet it may be sweet (4)
10 Investigation reaches wrong outcome after right start (8)
12 Mother's pets are dogs (8)
14 Used by riders but not as riding breeches (10)
16 Riding school discipline is a habit that comes with time (8)
17 They fly to Riva as a change (8)
19 Pet journal distributed around the first of May (6)
20 Private line to the Queen? (6)
22 Secured the same numbers of points? (4)
23 Chinese capital lies in total waste (4)

70

ACROSS

1 Tough at the top? (4-6)
6 Girl back in Hammersmith (4)
10 Go over again for engineers' headgear (5)
11 Mischievous person is married to violence (9)
12 Girl opening place for women in black (7)
13 Saunter'd round without an article in a small place in Somerset (7)
14 A picture for example (12)
18 Looking after number one on holiday? (4-8)
21 Got up late! (7)
23 An ostensible reason was given before the Biblical passage (7)
24 The same small car may be for the friar (9)
25 Contribution from trendy set (5)
26 Pipe was put under water, it was announced (4)
27 Ray listing elements causing inflammation (10)

DOWN

1 Man finding a chore upsetting (6)
2 Modern design centre (6)
3 Phi's operation (3,11)
4 Not in favour of a group of commercial enterprises regulating monopolies (9)
5 Made a mistake in Dover reducing the price (5)
7 Defend keep (8)
8 Having high opinion of crazy maid with small hoop (8)
9 People engaged in this feel on top of the world (14)
15 One who was eager for profit had to go round with very little money (4-5)
16 Rose on the throne? (8)
17 Michael removing copyright concerning an infant state of chemistry (8)

19 Brewer's receptacle (6)
20 It is to exacerbate the inflammation (6)
22 Did I catch them always initially making up formal sayings? (5)

71

ACROSS

7 Stay and have a glass of ale (9)
8 Old Greek offering tip-top accommodation (5)
10 Quietly receive change for note (8)
11 Beast of burden carrying a grating (6)
12 Savage cut (4)
13 Exerting oneself with some point making records (8)
15 Permit to break silence (7)
17 A wool-gatherer making outrageous charges? (7)
20 Judgement given in a few words (8)
22 Some are bound over, some set free (4)
25 He knows his onions, parking a vehicle in the street (6)
26 Declining to be reasonable about sales-pitch (8)
27 Yank's spirit (5)
28 Concerns trendy testers-out (9)

DOWN

1 Figure employer is a thoughtful person (5)
2 Pop back hurt but brave (6)
3 Made up for the press – badly, it's clear (8)
4 Touching lines, or just the opposite? (7)
5 In exceptional situation the Left put the squeeze on (8)
6 One repudiating the new residents' association (9)
9 The love of a man (4)
14 Settling bill early in big-hearted way (9)
16 Access may be used when transport's wanted (8)
18 Took a meal without any starter, and pushed off (8)
19 Principal member occupied by a big row (7)
21 Mark has school backing (4)
23 Sharp practices of an artful Dickensian character? (6)

24 A girl from Milan – Italian of course (5)

72

ACROSS

1 Shriek from engineers caught in swindle (6)
5 Amazing chap hiding in Kent (8)
9 Call to resume fight: unconscious after less than a minute (7,3)
10 Hello, sailor! (4)
11 Spontaneity of solicitor's generous offer? (4,4)
12 Distant meteor crashed (6)
13 Talented contribution to tableau (4)
15 Boring partner who lives with you? (8)
18 Last product, probably not a single one sold (8)
19 Decide what to do with a little money (4)
21 We hear bloke is one that spouts regularly (6)
23 Halo of light over this port? (8)
25 Parting gesture from one on the sea (4)
26 Stuck up a couple of rhymes (5-5)
27 With wild rage, give distress (8)
28 Make smaller and subdue (6)

DOWN

2 Wholly vindicate (5)
3 Unauthorised rush to join union (9)
4 It is really crazy to free capital (6)
5 Cannot decide whether it has been ruined deliberately? (6,3,6)
6 It's safe to criticise one who never grows up (5,3)
7 Genuine mark made by kingdom (5)
8 At sea, stop trouble from rats (9)
14 Weapon dispersed Orange mob (9)
16 Rival deal that is in splinters (9)
17 What does cashmere come from? I really have no idea! (6,2)
20 Competitor takes quiet course (6)
22 Vow to profane (5)
24 A teetotaller in charge of lofty area (5)

73

ACROSS

1 Better take a leisurely walk in Greece (7)
5 To track round Virginia requires great effort (7)
9 Aim to be impartial (9)
10 "Uneasy lies the head that wears a —— "
Shakespeare's *Henry IV* (5)
11 Get back into the centre of the train (7)
12 Really weary solicitor full of fury (4,3)
13 Bound to replace bloated GI (9)
16 One large cat is bony (5)
17 Coppers put enclosure in front of church (5)
18 Further comments made by chiropodists? (9)
21 Feature otherwise displayed by Judas (7)
22 It gives light instrument a lining of mesh (7)
25 Old Mrs Merrilies gets a letter from Athens (5)
26 Firm statement that treason is corrupt (9)
27 Enforce law if a street is in disrepair (7)
28 Remedy for a broken banjo? (7)

DOWN

1 Marx used to grumble over nothing (7)
2 No minor member of a previous administration (5)
3 In Honolulu crewman carry cash (5)
4 Intend to get into torn clothing (7)
5 Negotiated to be given medication (7)
6 Instrument of agreement, upsetting no-one (9)
7 US soldiers take time to support a game defender (9)
8 A heavyweight not short on style (4,3)
14 Farm manager must bring a toff down to earth (4-5)
15 Enraged at being mauled by a hound (5,4)
17 Patrick Moore loses heart to English poet (7)
18 A king in banquet, from China, maybe (3,4)
19 So nylon is manufactured by sole male heir (4,3)

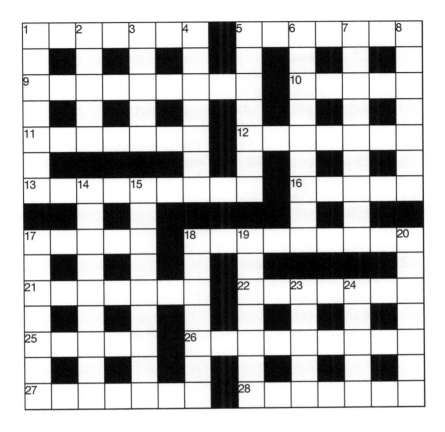

20 Severe hesitation to reveal the breastbone (7)
23 Annoys informers (5)
24 He attempts to get right into row (5)

74

ACROSS

1 Audience left part of theatre (5,5)
9 Go back always to this portraitist (4)
10 Advise colleague in unofficial manner (10)
11 Seek profit, having lost one's shirt? (6)
12 Lecturer holds I must be better prepared (7)
15 Circle lake, being after somewhere to sleep (7)
16 This Italian capital fellow (5)
17 Musical animals (4)
18 Well-liked, but expensive (4)
19 To be of use, verse must be translated (5)
21 Fan has a look at large animal (7)
22 Once modelled naked (7)
24 Book about business is on the way (2,4)
27 The worst-looking person in Coventry? (7,3)
28 Gem friend added to ring (4)
29 An irrelevance that her grinder is broken (3,7)

DOWN

2 Military vehicle found in reservoir (4)
3 Gravitational acceleration about the Earth (6)
4 Walker rose (7)
5 Little girl has a quantity of spirits (4)
6 Take a liberty and use the fitting room (3,2,2)
7 Morse's role redesigned, sort of (4,2,4)
8 Bars putting a limit on range of stock (6-4)
12 Worst possible seat when music's on (4,6)
13 Dreadful liar, if I act false (10)
14 Typical lover, more upset about love (5)
15 Cut right into hollow feature (5)
19 Unsuspected spy in railway compartment (7)
20 Check river has a minimum content (7)
23 Animal chewed orange (6)
25 Plummet from first place (4)
26 Show disapproval of new benefit (4)

75

ACROSS

1 An ironclad reason for not buying luxuries (8)
6 Girl knocked out, in coma (6)
9 Back payment for an artist (6)
10 One caught in the very act of stealing (8)
11 Battle station (8)
12 Unbridled lust, an essential for an Eastern ruler (6)
13 Digital recordings? (12)
16 Snacks for new students in rest break (12)
19 Journalist's turn to ride (6)
21 Choice way of take sustenance (1,2,5)
23 At this point, land appears (3-5)
24 How to amuse motorists? Hardly! (6)
25 Sound move, plain to a Russian (6)
26 Furtive sort of hat style (8)

DOWN

2 Fresh air – and that's essential for a man (6)
3 Look for water to plunge into (5)
4 They give actors difficulty – what a shame! (4,5)
5 A job for the tinker on the way (7)
6 Posts a slim package (5)
7 Work of fiction joins together strange things (9)
8 Dog goes mad for fruit (8)
13 Cricketer's initial mistake? (5,4)
14 With bowl, manage to beg (9)
15 Preliminary race which is neither quick nor decisive (4,4)
17 Some rash German, perhaps (7)
18 Carbohydrate consumed makes clothes hard to wear (6)
20 Show regret about evening being cut short (5)
22 It's hard hit when ironworkers strike (5)

76

ACROSS

1 Pass Cumbrian town using a light cart (10)
6 A fair I missed at a remote spot (4)
9 Recover consciousness, nothing less, to see the heavenly body (5)
10 Slavered, having talked nonsense (9)
12 Nostril found in the ice? (9-4)
14 Not, say, the company to assert positively again (8)
15 Fellow model takes one's small creature (6)
17 Remove whitewash from French bed (6)
19 Many an accountant taken in by feeble-minded person, one from Africa (8)
21 Last to the end of a boxing-match, or a race? (2,3,8)
24 An illuminating cover-up (9)
25 New diets, that is to say (2,3)
26 Still I follow the creature in the mountains (4)
27 From all quarters, landlord receives informal report (10)

DOWN

1 House has odd bits of cake and wine (4)
2 Main revolution by one taken in by scholar in the country (7)
3 One lets things drop (13)
4 Songster a bright colour to begin with (8)
5 Beat ruined biro, I concluded (5)
7 Do not agree that it could be dangerous (4,3)
8 Making up for changing one's clothes? (10)
11 Encourage cold sauce to be put on a dish (3,10)
13 Wastefully in a manner like Luke's son (10)
16 Lock for leading defence (8)
18 Where one can stand out of the wet (4-3)
20 A kind man? (7)
22 I'm taking time to produce a likeness (5)

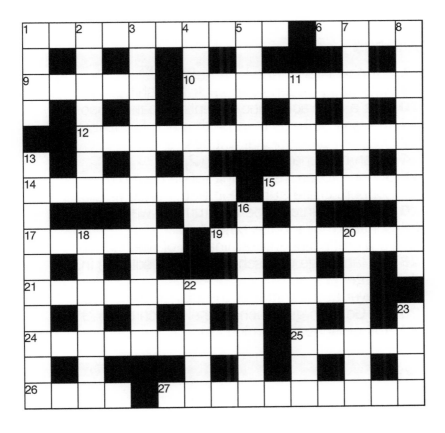

23 Mix thoroughly in jug (4)

77

ACROSS

1 Put down iron in the long grass (9)
9 Note half-a-dozen keep back – so shifty (7)
10 He's a poor actor who accepts female support (7)
11 Tea isn't perhaps taken with much formality (2,5)
12 Drag out professional writings (9)
14 Mean it to change? Never! (2,2,4)
15 Sound procedure needing refinement (6)
17 Coppers chafe at being in attendance (7)
20 Make certain of dope and running water (6)
23 Contest that's in the bag (4,4)
25 To air reflection in examination of rhetoric (9)
26 The language of a scholar held by soldiers in charge! (7)
27 Forever at the throat of the man in the office (7)
28 The German girl teaching the French one (7)
29 Fruit crushes aren't nice (9)

DOWN

2 A hold-up caused by mob rage (7)
3 About the current height for the power-station (7)
4 Refits are safer for the sailing man (8)
5 To stay in the Hebrides is the thing! (6)
6 Go away without games and travel-documents (9)
7 Giant takes first-class return to see the queen (7)
8 The judge should admit a point many mention (9)
13 Dicky tarries, the little beast! (7)
15 A painter pores over a catalogue (9)
16 What's left in black may be worn (9)
18 The most unpalatable wine is acceptable in the home (8)
19 The City retreats offering cakes (7)
21 He refuses to work, yet makes a favourable impression (7)
22 Get into a row – not for the first time (7)

24 Money placed outside the church in India (6)

78

ACROSS

1 Pool made by young cat (5)
4 Night-club certain to upset conversation (9)
9 Startle birds out and about (with no ring fitted) (7)
11 A dairy product one meets on border (7)
12 A big hit over centre-line (4)
13 Deposit for a cottage (5)
14 Announce piece of legislation (4)
17 Soldier hear plain order to find things (13)
19 The new stadium constructed for a football club? (4,3,6)
21 Science article to study (4)
22 Making way in dried grass produces rash (5)
23 Hollow warning (4)
26 Bond to hit wine (7)
27 Old measure of land by the ton (7)
28 Regard tip oddly – particularly one given at Christmas (9)
29 Mockingly, he is said to have an easy life (5)

DOWN

1 Leather finally chosen for backing novel (9)
2 Better half drinks Italian wine, it's more palatable (7)
3 What has replaced "thy" and "thou" – right? (4)
5 Informal language in key fixture – vituperative exchange (8,5)
6 Nothing the matter with work (4)
7 Greek wine retains liquid (7)
8 Loner travelling to join up? (5)
10 Sorrowful composition of Bartok end here, unexpectedly? (13)
15 Soft mass treated – now fit! (5)
16 Black Country is mild (5)
18 Woeful time for new deliveries (9)

19 Cover for the present, in case? (7)
20 One carries things on it – about four? (3,4)
21 Bit of a row (5)
24 Inferior quality of gold found at bottom of river (4)
25 Small present at Christmas perhaps (4)

79

ACROSS

1 He demands money for a huge platter (7)
5 Corporation has reservation getting Dutch currency (7)
9 Claimed to have been a success (4,3)
10 Executed about fifty after being ousted (7)
11 Fanciful description of Tinker Bell? (4-5)
12 Casual worker goes to eastern Greek valley (5)
13 Timely indication of stress (5)
15 Not informed that candles are needed (2,3,4)
17 Handy replacement of a garden shrub! (9)
19 Understood by Irish leader involved in diplomacy (5)
22 Blast! No relish! (5)
23 Model fellow born one of five (9)
25 Rex meets Virginia in rigorous US university (7)
26 A job offered to the French missionary (7)
27 Sets are distributed in mosaic (7)
28 "I am not come to —— , but to fulfil"(*St Matthew's Gospel*) (7)

DOWN

1 Brief agreement (7)
2 Director coming in soon to get a firedog (7)
3 Cease to function and leave (2,3)
4 Passing on gossip is a shopkeeper's job (9)
5 Manage to squeeze past (3,2)
6 Eager to make me paint it (9)
7 Putting cover back on Austen novel is a problem (7)
8 American white infuriated by left-wing audacity (7)
14 To give further details is complicated (9)
16 What the conductor does for old citizen soldiers (9)
17 Only a snob wants a topper (4,3)
18 The wishes of French fathers (7)
20 Token for a teller (7)
21 Produced yarn, net and leather there (7)

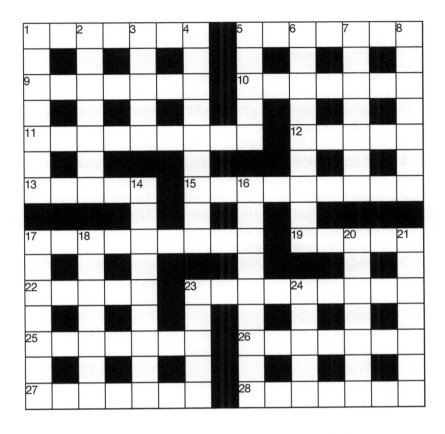

23 News channels in an old Asian country (5)
24 No sex maniac released by Yeoman officers (5)

ACROSS

1 Sat tying bib, perhaps, doing this job? (4-7)
7 Requires pounds, say (5)
8 Against going to tennis ground where we beat the French once (9)
10 Globe – that's necessary to see (7)
11 Discussed action to guard protected mammal (7)
12 Left before the recess – an oversight (5)
13 Dating from long ago, Lancaster was broken up (9)
16 Guard only temporarily in charge (9)
18 Shout half-heartedly downstairs (5)
19 Not many mistake good for bad, for example (7)
22 Society woman's husband was US commander (7)
23 Financial officer is an invaluable servant, right? (9)
24 Naturally, mass movements mainly have their ups and downs (5)
25 Formal coat in which to attend *Madam Butterfly*? (11)

DOWN

1 His charges may be stinging, but his workers are devoted to the queen (3-6)
2 Part of the way not to be covered by car? (3-4)
3 Stride round shopping precinct, having a chat (5-4)
4 Had a go at judging? (5)
5 One new baby to us is a nightmare (7)
6 Sound from pig at last, the smallest one (5)
7 Embroidery showing an Isle of Wight pleasure boat? (11)
9 This flipping game is going to pot (11)
14 It's my turn to open some wine (9)
15 In part, one sets a good example (4,5)
17 In a suit, travel to the country (7)
18 Just the drink to strengthen one with a complaint? (4,3)

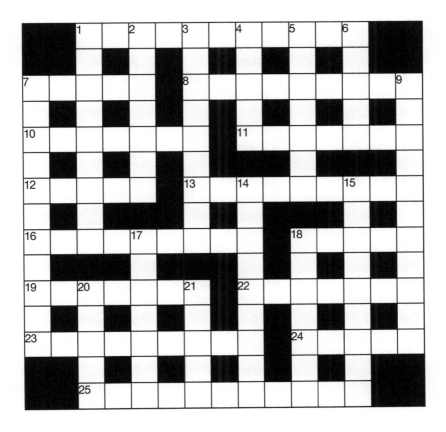

20 Lock of hair Bill snipped from starlet (5)
21 Mark spoken lesson (5)

ANSWERS

1

Across
1 Housebound
6 Gong
9 Sonneteers
10 Deaf
13 Visited
15 Barsac
16 Didcot
17 Exclamation mark
18 Tassel
20 Aragon
21 Depress
22 Abib
25 Edward Lear
26 Land
27 Protestant

Down
1 Hash
2 Ulna
3 Edenic
4 Obedient servant
5 Narked
7 Overcharge
8 Gift tokens
11 Object ball
12 Procession
13 Vacated
14 Dinners
19 Leader
20 Asides
23 Feta
24 Fret

2

Across
7 Cat and dog
8 Tenby
10 Doorknob
11 Abacus
12 Edda
13 Locality
16 Teak
18 Egghead
20 Academy
22 Amyl
24 Gruesome
26 Abba
29 Avalon
30 Lambaste
31 Stash
32 Wednesday

Down
1 Havoc
2 Madrid
3 Edentata
4 Tombola
5 Recalled
6 About time
9 Laic
14 Okay
15 Aggravate
17 Edam
19 Heedless
21 Claimant
23 Mealies
25 Owns
27 Braise
28 Steal

3

Across
1 Glanced
5 Sweep up
9 Drilling machine
10 Exam
11 Title
12 Etui
15 Scenery
16 Stomach
17 Pickled
19 A bit off
21 Rare
22 Uhlan
23 Etna
26 Woody nightshade
27 Ganders
28 Sweater

Down
1 Gadgets
2 Animated cartoon
3 Calf
4 Density
5 Samples
6 Each
7 Paints a portrait
8 Peevish
13 Veils
14 Yogin
17 Periwig
18 Dahlias
19 Apaches
20 Flaneur
24 Hyde
25 Ashe

4

Across

1 Air Sea Rescue
8 Ana
9 Tabloid
11 Elderly
12 Dead-eye
13 Caned
14 Idle hands
16 Languidly
18 Paean
20 Unloose
22 Ermined
23 Schools
25 Bow
26 Army exercise

Down

1 Abandon
2 Retired
3 Early bird
4 Rated
5 Sabbath
6 Ufo
7 Watercolours
10 Dressing down
15 Lay reader
17 Ufology
18 Pompeii
19 Ennoble
21 Essex
24 Her

5

Across

1 Hugger-mugger
8 Lobster
9 Toothed
11 Batsman
12 Facades
13 Oaten
14 Candidate
16 Easterner
19 Poilu
21 Humdrum
23 Impresa
24 Rerated
25 Set sail
26 Firm measures

Down

1 Habitat
2 Gateman
3 Eirenicon
4 Motif
5 Gnocchi
6 Echidna
7 Club together
10 Disreputable
15 Narcissus
17 Samurai
18 Erratum
19 Pop star
20 Icecaps
22 Midge

6

Across

1 Real estate
6 Otho
9 Cabal
10 Debatable
12 Tatters
13 Moron
15 Blow out
17 Origami
19 Dashing
21 Aintree
22 Envoi
24 Abaddon
27 Tonbridge
28 Raree
29 Yale
30 Interceded

Down

1 Race
2 Albatross
3 Eclat
4 Tidiest
5 Tabasco
7 Tiber
8 Ocean liner
11 Tompion
14 Obediently
16 Olivier
18 Aaron's rod
20 Gladden
21 Academe
23 Venal
25 Doric
26 Feud

7

Across
1 Long run
5 Dadaist
9 Teachable
10 Depot
11 Eliza
12 Bridewell
13 Yardstick
16 Chair
17 Ducal
18 Christian
20 Macaronic
23 Proem
25 Garda
26 Earlier on
27 Descent
28 Optical

Down
1 Lathery
2 Naafi
3 Rehearsal
4 Nabob
5 Die sinker
6 Dodge
7 Impresari
8 Tattler
14 Race cards
15 In concert
16 Cash point
17 Damaged
19 Nominal
21 Reade
22 Cargo
24 Osric

8

Across
1 Inelegant
9 Bureau
10 Idealists
11 Open up
12 In general
13 Kismet
17 Fly
19 Macabre
20 Abutted
21 Elk
23 Laredo
27 Abundance
28 Archer
29 Dress suit
30 Maraca
31 Emanation

Down
2 Nadine
3 Leader
4 Glider
5 Netball
6 Bumptious
7 Re-animate
8 Turpitude
14 Small arms
15 Score card
16 Obedience
17 Fee
18 Yak
22 Labarum
24 Unison
25 Basset
26 Schizo

9

Across
1 North star
9 Erosion
10 Sketchy
11 Eskdale
12 Grenadier
14 Beam ends
15 Teasel
17 Beaters
20 Astral
23 Labelled
25 Aerialist
26 Leering
27 Lenient
28 Absence
29 Sassenach

Down
2 Oak tree
3 Tetanus
4 Schedule
5 Revere
6 Look a mess
7 Sixaine
8 Under seal
13 Ebbtide
15 Table leaf
16 Ebullient
18 Raciness
19 Abreast
21 Tallinn
22 Arsenic
24 Eagles

10

Across
4 Pacifist
8 Elaine
9 In camera
10 Jack it in
11 Abduct
12 Mesdames
13 Adoption
16 Graffito
19 Raillery
21 Forest
23 Rainless
24 Victoria
25 Elands
26 Ashplant

Down
1 Bleared
2 Ticked off
3 Septum
4 Paints a portrait
5 Cachalot
6 Famed
7 Sirocco
14 Table leaf
15 Wistaria
17 Rookies
18 Crusade
20 Ibidem
22 Estop

11

Across
1 Germicidal
6 Raki
10 Earls
11 Paramorph
12 Bean pole
13 Nodal
15 In range
17 Subject
19 Unhappy
21 Theorbo
22 Dowel
24 Camellia
27 Supporter
28 Nerve
29 Ride
30 Brandy snap

Down
1 Gael
2 Rare earth
3 Ibsen
4 Implore
5 Airless
7 Aired
8 Inhalation
9 Amenable
14 Liquidiser
16 Napoleon
18 Earlier on
20 Yachter
21 Tamarin
23 Wiped
25 Lanky
26 Heap

12

Across
1 Lurked
5 Macaroni
9 Copenhagen
10 Crew
11 Ptomaine
12 Darwin
13 Rant
15 Imagines
18 Pathetic
19 Ease
21 Aragon
23 Make a hit
25 Menu
26 Rhapsodies
27 Platypus
28 Serbia

Down
2 U-boat
3 Keen match
4 Dahlia
5 Magnetic compass
6 Canadian
7 Racer
8 Neediness
14 A fair deal
16 Icelander
17 Eton crop
20 Ukases
22 Gaunt
24 Iceni

13

Across
1 Gamester
5 Osbert
9 Back pack
10 Cresta
12 Lie low
13 Table mat
15 Beagles
16 Unco
20 Read
21 Fielder
25 Psalmist
26 Egg cup
28 Smudge
29 Reveille
30 Latest
31 Turned in

Down
1 Gabble
2 Mickey
3 Supposed
4 Etch
6 Stroll
7 Easy mind
8 Traction
11 Eagerly
14 Against
17 Proposal
18 Paraquat
19 Pea-green
22 Images
23 Scaled
24 Spleen
27 Beau

14

Across
1 Rustler
5 Periwig
9 Benders
10 Apparel
11 Idle hands
12 Chose
13 Sassy
15 Ice hockey
17 Asparagus
19 Sinai
22 Icons
23 Buckhound
25 Ocarina
26 Alberta
27 Frankly
28 Tattles

Down
1 Rabbits
2 Singles
3 Leech
4 Resenting
5 Peals
6 Rapacious
7 Warlock
8 Gallery
14 Yardstick
16 East coast
17 A bit off
18 Pro rata
20 Neutral
21 Indians
23 Beady
24 Habit

15

Across
1 Oyster plant
9 Afar
10 Sleep walker
11 Gean
14 Fret saw
16 Sea bass
17 Lager
18 Eels
19 Shot
20 Pedal
22 Tackier
23 Nacelle
24 Tail
28 Allegorical
29 Oink
30 Grease paint

Down
2 Yale
3 Tael
4 Raw deal
5 Loll
6 Needier
7 After awhile
8 Trend setter
12 Affectation
13 Reflections
15 Wafer
16 Sedan
20 Pearler
21 Lactose
25 Bema
26 Diva
27 Caen

16

Across

1 Tympanum
5 Odessa
9 Bad taste
10 Used up
11 Radio ham
12 Hot air
14 Journeymen
18 Ingredient
22 Laical
23 Fearless
24 Eagles
25 Demerara
26 Sanity
27 Close tie

Down

1 Tabard
2 Made do
3 Amazon
4 Ultrasonic
6 Discover
7 Side arms
8 Apparent
13 Orange peel
15 Fielders
16 Egging on
17 Decadent
19 Briefs
20 Pedant
21 Escape

17

Across

5 Batman
8 Immersed
9 Sloe gin
10 Elcho
11 Dachshund
13 Teetotal
14 Aerate
17 Ian
19 Odd
20 Medici
23 Trollope
26 Trousseau
28 Eerie
29 Amatory
30 Stashing
31 Andrew

Down

1 Nicest
2 Smacker
3 Ergonomic
4 Nevada
5 Bald head
6 Teeth
7 Alienate
12 Alb
15 Edelweiss
16 Merry men
18 Air-screw
21 Eta
22 No train
24 Rubato
25 Emerge
27 Utter

18

Across

1 Bartenders
9 Memo
10 Peppermill
11 Aghast
12 Poppets
15 Pianola
16 Eaten
17 Dace
18 Sera
19 Court
21 In a spot
22 Yearned
24 Grieve
27 Take in hand
28 Oche
29 Cleaner air

Down

2 Apex
3 Tiptop
4 Narrate
5 Evil
6 Saladin
7 Get a move on
8 Contraband
12 Paddington
13 Pick a fight
14 Sabot
15 Perry
19 Cometic
20 Tension
23 Rasher
25 Skye
26 Anti

19

Across
1 Conventional
9 Shuffle
10 Suffolk
11 Late
12 On air
13 Diet
16 Tacitly
17 Gold nib
18 Oatmeal
21 Hosanna
23 Iago
24 Tiara
25 Aced
28 Tally-ho
29 Nankeen
30 Agree to terms

Down
1 Caustic
2 Naff
3 Epernay
4 Tasting
5 Oafs
6 Aeolian
7 Isolationists
8 Skateboarding
14 Uther
15 Blast
19 Tagalog
20 Laid out
21 Horn-nut
22 Nucleus
26 Gyve
27 Knar

20

Across
7 Slap happy
8 Mug up
10 Ananas
11 Ear piece
12 Crimea
14 Uptown
16 Alas
17 Aired
18 Gift
19 Duenna
21 Nature
24 Ligature
26 Agatha
27 Alibi
28 Scale down

Down
1 Glint
2 Open arms
3 Balsam
4 Epee
5 Nudist
6 Dutch wife
9 Around
13 Aaron
15 Plausible
17 Abacus
18 Garlands
20 Nearby
22 Teazle
23 Shawl
25 Etch

21

Across
1 Apprentice
9 Emir
10 Centigrade
11 Roll up
12 Apostle
15 Blowfly
16 Yield
17 Ties
18 Free
19 Deeds
21 Nattier
22 Earshot
24 Sleeve
27 Run-through
28 Eton
29 Shillelagh

Down
2 Peep
3 Ratios
4 Nightly
5 Iran
6 Emerald
7 Ampleforth
8 Prepayment
12 Astonishes
13 Over the top
14 Eider
15 Blade
19 Deserts
20 Satchel
23 School
25 Anti
26 Agog

22

Across
1 Cut-price
5 Pelmet
10 Miserable sinner
11 Baghdad
12 Garland
13 Consider
15 Macaw
18 Paper
20 Co-worker
23 Officer
25 Sugared
26 King of the forest
27 Trying
28 Enclosed

Down
1 Come by
2 Task-group
3 Reredos
4 Cubed
6 Epigram
7 Manna
8 Turn down
9 Hedgerow
14 Decorate
16 Cheerless
17 Sprocket
19 Raccoon
21 Ragdoll
22 Edited
24 Fancy
25 Stern

23

Across
5 Pigeon
8 As long as
9 Stories
10 Teach
11 Tolerable
13 Reversed
14 Impair
17 Say
19 Ace
20 Stress
23 Patients
26 Glistened
28 Adage
29 Rangoon
30 Director
31 Stated

Down
1 Raptor
2 Algarve
3 Anchoress
4 Canute
5 Pathetic
6 Gerda
7 Overlaid
12 Odd
15 Medicated
16 Stalwart
18 Asteroid
21 Ape
22 Infanta
24 Adonis
25 Sherry
27 Sight

24

Across
1 Talent
4 Corsairs
9 Ornate
10 Debonair
12 Lima
13 Crept
14 Sump
17 Perambulator
20 Ecclesiastes
23 Plan
24 Ambit
25 Dodo
28 Archduke
29 Genius
30 Glossary
31 Ordeal

Down
1 Trollope
2 Landmark
3 Note
5 Oneupmanship
6 Slow
7 Icarus
8 Scrape
11 Troublemaker
15 Smack
16 Foray
18 Atropine
19 Espousal
21 Sprang
22 Gaucho
26 Ides
27 Wear

25

Across

7 Get away
8 Calibre
10 Lock-keeper
11 Tick
12 Terrapin
14 Odessa
15 Taken to task
19 Make up
20 Rounds on
22 Stet
23 Reflection
25 Brother
26 Ashamed

Down

1 Demoted
2 Back
3 Take up
4 Carry out
5 Distressed
6 Precise
9 Spendthrift
13 Real estate
16 Exporter
17 Battery
18 Boloney
21 Uneasy
24 Team

26

Across

1 Strip cartoon
9 Learner
10 Planter
11 Chip
12 Began
13 Vain
16 Angelus
17 Taunton
18 Digress
21 Lion cub
23 Harm
24 Purge
25 Para
28 Tea-time
29 Colossi
30 Tennis player

Down

1 Slaving
2 Rung
3 Perseus
4 Asphalt
5 Thai
6 Outcast
7 Black-and-white
8 Grin and bear it
14 Sleek
15 Tutor
19 Garbage
20 Saucers
21 Logical
22 Coarser
26 Finn
27 Slay

27

Across

1 Caper
4 Congreve
8 Abutment
9 Sediment
11 Hedonic
13 Alexander
15 Gift from the gods
18 Rehearsed
21 Emeriti
22 Soapsuds
24 Love knot
25 Beetroot
26 Ailed

Down

1 Coat hanger
2 Plum duff
3 Romanoff
4 Cots
5 Godiva
6 Exceed
7 Emit
10 Eventide
12 Caroused
14 Restricted
16 Ephemera
17 Optional
19 Hoarse
20 Answer
22 Scab
23 Slot

28

Across
1 Medick
4 Flashgun
10 Kings Lynn
11 Gland
12 Sabbath
13 Octagon
14 Rathe
15 Showdown
18 Consommé
20 Nylon
23 Cabinet
25 Freesia
26 Inter
27 Keeping on
28 Marching
29 Uneasy

Down
1 Make sure
2 Dingbat
3 Castanets
5 Land on one's feet
6 Sight
7 Glasgow
8 Nadine
9 By the same token
16 Dandelion
17 Ungainly
19 Orbiter
21 Lasagna
22 Schism
24 North

29

Across
1 Malefactor
6 Scab
10 Lined
11 Steadfast
12 Moderate
13 Panel
15 Absolve
17 Skipped
19 Cleaner
21 Senator
22 Eagle
24 Abeyance
27 Tea-cosies
28 At one
29 Rita
30 Stonemason

Down
1 Mole
2 Langouste
3 Fudge
4 Cascade
5 Oneness
7 Chain
8 Battledore
9 Adoption
14 Manchester
16 Lancelot
18 Put across
20 Realist
21 Stepson
23 Graft
25 Alarm
26 Penn

30

Across
1 As sound as a bell
9 Charity
10 Canasta
11 Sole
12 Permafrost
14 Decoct
15 Crackers
17 Tamboura
18 Combat
21 Cradle song
22 Blur
24 Initial
25 Grannie
26 Unpleasantness

Down
1 Accused
2 Stable companion
3 Unit
4 Dryden
5 Sycamore
6 Benefactor
7 Lose one's balance
8 Mantis
13 Schoolgirl
16 Brasilia
17 Tocsin
19 Targets
20 Enigma
23 Part

31

Across
1 Colander
9 In armour
10 Heir
11 Off the record
13 Butter up
15 Amulet
16 Peri
17 Class
18 Tear
20 Litmus
21 His Grace
23 New Hampshire
26 Nuts
27 Universe
28 Contrary

Down
2 Overture
3 Air of triumph
4 Duffer
5 Rich
6 Fairways
7 Logo
8 Creditor
12 Counter-tenor
14 Poach
16 Polonius
17 Costmary
19 Ancestor
22 Slip-on
24 Whip
25 Spec

32

Across
1 Bear with me
6 Asia
9 Obese
10 Limelight
12 Going for a song
14 Straw hat
15 Misfit
17 Eschew
19 Software
21 Bosworth Field
24 Apartment
25 Anvil
26 Even
27 Shrink-wrap

Down
1 Boob
2 Avenger
3 Week in week out
4 Telegram
5 Mambo
7 Sign off
8 Altogether
11 Leap in the dark
13 Assemblage
16 Confetti
18 Cascade
20 Andover
22 Teeth
23 Clip

33

Across
1 Grand finale
9 Bottoms up
10 Ruler
11 Old man
12 Insecure
13 Serbia
15 Misprint
18 Pathetic
19 Arnhem
21 Apostles
23 Artful
26 Heart
27 In any case
28 Make believe

Down
1 Gibbous
2 Acted
3 Drop a line
4 Inst
5 Appendix
6 Eerie
7 Garment
8 Flourish
14 Rational
16 Portrayal
17 Limerick
18 Peaches
20 Maltese
22 Totem
24 Frame
25 Lamb

34

Across
1 Icecap
5 Hill town
9 Tourniquet
10 Mask
11 Repartee
12 Amoeba
13 Cadi
15 Organist
18 Trinidad
19 Nina
21 Odessa
23 Retrench
25 Coil
26 Exorcising
27 Mephitis
28 Yonder

Down
2 Close
3 Carnation
4 Plinth
5 Household troops
6 Lethargy
7 Tempo
8 Washbasin
14 Aerodrome
16 Non-person
17 Adjacent
20 Sticky
22 Sylph
24 Canoe

35

Across
7 Wresting
9 Eleven
10 Odds
11 Parliament
12 Stupid
14 Noah's Ark
15 Reside
17 Strike
20 Arbitral
22 Banish
23 Upper crust
24 Mown
25 Stucco
26 Headless

Down
1 Creditor
2 Isis
3 Limpid
4 Hesitant
5 Permission
6 Meaner
8 Goring
13 Pestilence
16 Director
18 Elsewise
19 Plough
21 Repute
22 Batman
24 Mold

36

Across
1 Unbrace
5 Oafs
9 Administration
11 Waif
12 Plead
13 Okra
16 Nucleus
17 Trainee
18 Felt tip
20 Bad show
22 Late
23 Droll
24 Spae
27 Shock treatment
28 Inky
29 Treason

Down
2 Bad circulation
3 Axis
4 Edibles
5 Outcast
6 Fear
7 Concave
8 Kick in the pants
10 Owen
14 Lento
15 Daddy
18 Film set
19 Portray
20 Ballast
21 Weed
25 Akin
26 Smee

37

Across
1 Domination
6 Part
10 Chant
11 Argentina
12 Assyrian
13 Whelp
15 Heeling
17 Chancel
19 Set fair
21 Bull run
22 Exact
24 Slip-case
27 Tailoring
28 Voice
29 Nosh
30 Temperance

Down
1 Duck
2 Means test
3 Natty
4 Teasing
5 Organic
7 Alive
8 Trampoline
9 Snowball
14 Chesterton
16 Inaction
18 Christian
20 Respite
21 Bring up
23 Alias
25 Cover
26 Fête

38

Across
7 Have words
8 Tacit
10 Domain
11 Mainline
12 Fitter
14 Lowest
16 Anne
17 Tight
18 Hate
19 Gibbon
21 Livery
24 Impudent
26 So be it
27 State
28 Smuggling

Down
1 Baton
2 Sedative
3 Cornet
4 Adam
5 Callow
6 Minnesota
9 Billet
13 Regal
15 Infirmity
17 Tanner
18 Harebell
20 Bounty
22 Visage
23 Fiend
25 Tome

39

Across
1 In touch
5 Bring up
9 Puttied
10 On leave
11 Strong-box
12 Eddie
13 Endue
15 Unimpeded
17 Partridge
19 Rides
22 Timon
23 Cultivate
25 Hold out
26 Support
27 Desists
28 Deluded

Down
1 Impasse
2 Tutored
3 Union
4 Hidebound
5 Bronx
6 Ill temper
7 Guarded
8 Pretend
14 Erroneous
16 Idealised
17 Pitched
18 Romulus
20 Diamond
21 Sweated
23 Cites
24 Impel

40

Across
4 Tight fit
8 Ardour
9 In a jiffy
10 Androgen
11 Rather
12 Attorney
13 Dogsbody
16 Archives
19 Gold-rush
21 Butter
23 Insecure
24 Distress
25 Reduce
26 Ensnared

Down
1 Trinity
2 Sourdough
3 Aragon
4 Thinly disguised
5 Glad rags
6 Taint
7 Infield
14 Barracuda
15 Overbear
17 Reunion
18 Ostrich
20 Lustre
22 Titan

41

Across
1 Head-on
4 Scarcity
9 Saddle
10 Snowball
12 Part
13 Sated
14 Iago
17 Peanut butter
20 Choreography
23 Away
24 Asset
25 Knee
28 Crossbow
29 Godiva
30 Disperse
31 Desert

Down
1 Hosepipe
2 Alderman
3 Only
5 Confectioner
6 Rows
7 Isaiah
8 Yellow
11 Barbers' shops
15 Ought
16 Genre
18 Open fire
19 Typecast
21 Rancid
22 Canoes
26 Isle
27 Robe

42

Across
8 Spur
9 Ram
10 Europe
11 Angled
12 Omissive
13 Resisting arrest
15 Hangdog
17 Violent
20 Tied hand and foot
23 Popinjay
25 Ablaze
26 Cortez
27 Net
28 Nine

Down
1 Sponge
2 Grilling
3 Traditional jazz
4 Impound
5 Hesitation waltz
6 Eraser
7 Spiv
14 Sun
16 Ali
18 Lifeline
19 Eddying
21 Dainty
22 Oozing
24 Oboe

43

Across

1 Masseur
5 Chatter
9 Slashed
10 Resorts
11 Imperfect
12 Stall
13 Gorse
15 Sentience
17 Contender
19 Score
22 Utter
23 Statement
25 Shingle
26 Imitate
27 Lighter
28 Gravest

Down

1 Masking
2 Scamper
3 Esher
4 Redressed
5 Corot
6 Assassins
7 Terrain
8 Resolve
14 Eyebright
16 Narrating
17 Counsel
18 Nothing
20 Operate
21 Entreat
23 Shear
24 Erica

44

Across

1 Osteoarthritis
9 Gutters
10 Batavia
11 Nest
12 Birthrates
14 Cinema
15 Harridan
17 Perfecto
18 Medusa
21 King's Bench
22 Dido
24 Licence
25 Chianti
26 As clear as a bell

Down

1 Organic
2 Titus Andronicus
3 Over
4 Rustic
5 Habitual
6 Interbreed
7 Invited audience
8 Raisin
13 Impersonal
16 Et cetera
17 Pokily
19 Asocial
20 Acacia
23 Lira

45

Across

1 Travelling crane
9 Carnage
10 Mangoes
11 Lend a hand
12 Opera
13 Dead end
15 Charity
17 Botanic
19 Express
21 Ascot
23 Cease-fire
25 In a word
26 Presage
27 Get one's head down

Down

1 Tickled
2 Arran
3 El Alamein
4 Leeward
5 Nomadic
6 Canto
7 At one time
8 Ecstasy
14 Attic salt
16 Apprehend
17 Bracing
18 Cicadas
19 Example
20 Shebeen
22 Thorn
24 Imago

46

Across
1 Pasta
4 Man Friday
9 Shelter
11 Respite
12 Hold
13 Joker
14 Enid
17 Secretary bird
19 Scandalmonger
21 Clan
22 Gripe
23 Barn
26 Pillion
27 St Leger
28 Rotherham
29 Cowed

Down
1 Posthaste
2 Shellac
3 Anti
5 Nursery slopes
6 Rose
7 Deigned
8 Yield
10 Root and branch
15 Vegan
16 Pilot
18 Aaron's Rod
19 Scarlet
20 Glasgow
21 Caper
24 Vice
25 Bloc

47

Across
1 Mistaken
6 Upbeat
9 Spirit
10 Sediment
11 Snowshoe
12 Rescue
13 Constituency
16 Danger signal
19 Hybrid
21 Sapphire
23 Boat race
24 Nelson
25 Allege
26 Tortoise

Down
2 Impend
3 Threw
4 Kitchener
5 Nascent
6 Under
7 Bombshell
8 Announce
13 Cigarette
14 Tin opener
15 Baby doll
17 Inspect
18 Errors
20 Drake
22 Hello

48

Across
1 Account rendered
9 Replanted
10 Amiss
11 Oilskin
12 Whitsun
13 Ire
14 Druidic
17 Despair
19 Towrope
22 Drive-in
24 Nee
25 Omitted
26 Spanish
28 Inter
29 Overheads
30 Gone With The Wind

Down
1 Air-conditioning
2 Copal
3 Unasked
4 Titanic
5 Endowed
6 Diaries
7 Reinstate
8 Disenfranchised
15 Unwritten
16 Imp
18 Err
20 Outgrow
21 Endmost
22 Descent
23 Ivanhoe
27 Iraqi

49

Across

7 Firedamp
9 Opened
10 Acre
11 Depression
12 Supply
14 Idolater
15 Turner
17 Hearts
20 Reporter
22 Lagoon
23 Rationally
24 Cape
25 Debate
26 Erectors

Down

1 Discount
2 Cede
3 Hardly
4 Come come
5 Persian rug
6 Depose
8 Pops in
13 Periodical
16 Extended
18 Shoppers
19 Grille
21 Evader
22 Laymen
24 Cite

50

Across

1 Fishy
4 Hopscotch
8 Ready
9 Local time
11 Wage
12 Using
13 Skua
16 Inadvertently
19 Standard gauge
20 Lead
22 Girth
23 Bent
26 Esperanto
27 Realm
28 Secateurs
29 Waken

Down

1 Fireworks
2 Shangri-La
3 Yo-yo
4 Half-sovereign
5 Cold
6 Think
7 Hyena
10 Congregations
14 Hardy
15 Beaux
17 Theme park
18 Yachtsman
20 Leeds
21 Aspic
24 Grit
25 Draw

51

Across

1 Piece together
7 Set to
8 Bantering
9 Fitting
10 Play out
11 Tinge
12 Demitasse
14 Many-sided
17 Aware
19 Towards
21 Evil eye
22 Head-dress
23 Amend
24 Smelling salts

Down

1 Put it on
2 Emotive
3 Own up
4 Elegant
5 Heinous
6 Right Reverend
7 Safety matches
8 Baghdad
13 Madness
15 Newgate
16 Strudel
17 Abigail
18 Ageless
20 Stern

52

Across
1 Nuthatch
5 Confab
9 Dustcart
10 Dear me
12 Fruitcake
13 Swift
14 Wink
16 Trickle
19 Lucifer
21 Silk
24 Mourn
25 Major-domo
27 Tragic
28 Butchers
29 Stewed
30 Infringe

Down
1 Nod off
2 Tissue
3 Ascot
4 Car-park
6 Overspill
7 For kicks
8 Breathed
11 Belt
15 Infantile
17 Clematis
18 Accurate
20 Rime
21 Sojourn
22 Come on
23 Mousse
26 Recur

53

Across
1 Forbear
5 Inherit
9 Regally
10 Artiste
11 Donatello
12 Notes
13 Guyed
15 Ascertain
17 Life style
19 Natal
22 Their
23 Take leave
25 Referee
26 Ailment
27 Palette
28 Excuses

Down
1 Firedog
2 Regency
3 Eclat
4 Royal Navy
5 Idaho
6 Hit-and-run
7 Rosetta
8 Treason
14 Desert Rat
16 Checkmate
17 Lets rip
18 Fretful
20 Traders
21 Laertes
23 Theme
24 Lilac

54

Across
7 & 8 Salt of the earth
10 Asthma
11 Manicure
12 Meadow
14 Veleta
16 Writ
17 Got on
18 Show
19 Stormy
21 Yawing
24 Anaconda
26 Skinny
27 & 28 Henry the Eighth

Down
1 & 15 False pretences
2 Itchiest
3 Afraid
4 Sham
5 Parcel
6 & 23 At a rate of knots
9 Uneven
13 Withy
15 See 1
17 Guyana
18 Santiago
20 Record
22 Washer
23 See 6
25 Ache

55

Across
1 Relation
5 Scarab
9 Cataract
10 Mental
11 Rendered
12 Stoops
14 Stationary
18 Seasonably
22 Hebrew
23 Schooner
24 Doctor
25 Fiddling
26 Longed
27 Reverent

Down
1 Record
2 Latent
3 Turner
4 Orchestras
6 Creation
7 Rational
8 Bull's eye
13 Stalactite
15 Asphodel
16 Barbican
17 Borecole
19 Noodle
20 Entice
21 Fright

56

Across
1 Agent
4 Tetragram
8 Opera
9 Abseiling
11 Iota
12 Astir
13 Song
16 Anglo-American
19 Non-contagious
20 Test
22 Madam
23 Semi
26 Twentieth
27 Stops
28 Extractor
29 Dregs

Down
1 Abolition
2 Eyestrain
3 Trap
4 Transport café
5 Axis
6 Rhino
7 Magog
10 Seismographer
14 Aglow
15 Groom
17 Casserole
18 Narcissus
20 Tithe
21 Smelt
24 Etna
25 Used

57

Across
1 Butcher
5 Allowed
9 Minimal
10 Run into
11 Sling
12 Ascertain
13 Dormant
14 Tail-end
16 Abridge
19 Rambled
22 Acquitted
24 Diane
25 Animate
26 Abashed
27 Thereat
28 Speeded

Down
1 Bemused
2 Tangier
3 Home Guard
4 Reliant
5 Apricot
6 Loner
7 Wingate
8 Drowned
15 Immediate
16 Adamant
17 Require
18 Entreat
19 Redcaps
20 Leashed
21 Dreaded
23 Irate

58

Across

1 Martinet
6 Dismal
9 Corset
10 Interest
11 Pinafore
12 Sahara
13 Peak district
16 Christmas Eve
19 Concur
21 Overstep
23 Mistrust
24 At ease
25 Penned
26 Eternity

Down

2 Adonis
3 Tosca
4 Not so fast
5 Tail-end
6 Dates
7 Surcharge
8 Abstract
13 Princeton
14 Stevenage
15 Theorise
17 Apostle
18 Bed-sit
20 Round
22 Stern

59

Across

1 Headland
9 In a flash
10 Beef
11 Fills the bill
13 Teardrop
15 Lancer
16 Mean
17 Stair
18 Seen
20 Indigo
21 Debonair
23 Table manners
26 Tugs
27 Inclined
28 Endorsed

Down

2 Eye-piece
3 Differential
4 Antler
5 Digs
6 Bachelor
7 Bali
8 Children
12 Bend sinister
14 Plaid
16 Maintain
17 Stormont
19 Epilogue
22 Brewed
24 Buck
25 Nude

60

Across

1 Shackle
5 Utensil
9 Abandoned
10 Thora
11 Balsa
12 Earmarked
13 Xylophone
16 Corer
17 Truer
18 Antipodes
20 Nostalgia
23 Indus
25 Guava
26 Temporise
27 Teashop
28 Tangled

Down

1 Soapbox
2 Avail
3 Kidnapper
4 Ernie
5 Underfelt
6 Extra
7 Snookered
8 Leander
14 Louisiana
15 Orange-tip
16 Capricorn
17 Tonight
19 Suspend
21 Awash
22 Admit
24 Drill

61

Across
1 Switchboard
8 Odds and ends
11 Life
12 Each
13 Scoffed
15 Dwindle
16 Risen
17 Beeb
18 Tiff
19 Uglis
21 Othello
22 Teacher
23 Edam
26 Take
27 Devastation
28 Advertising

Down
2 Wade
3 Tastier
4 Hand
5 One down
6 Ride
7 Glass blower
8 Off one's head
9 Sandwich man
10 Sheep farmer
14 Dingo
15 Debit
19 Ululate
20 Sedates
24 Mead
25 Stet
26 Torn

62

Across
7 Alternate
8 Fable
10 Emanated
11 Indaba
12 Plan
13 Ugliness
15 Scalded
17 Effaced
20 Caprices
22 Eros
25 Hit out
26 Rabbitry
27 Snare
28 Unattired

Down
1 Alamo
2 Fennel
3 Instance
4 Stadium
5 Gardenia
6 Alabaster
9 Rill
14 Occasions
16 Larboard
18 Flea-bite
19 Tsarina
21 Cato
23 Origin
24 Treen

63

Across
1 Watershed
9 Abelard
10 Calibre
11 Bin
12 Mar
13 Adam's wine
15 Oddments
16 Enisle
18 Adamant
21 Aerate
24 Einstein
26 Oscillate
27 Nab
28 Red
29 Envelop
30 Steamed
31 Eagle-eyed

Down
2 Abaddon
3 Enigmas
4 Scrawled
5 Dabbed
6 Re-animate
7 Jamming
8 Addressee
14 Normans
16 Eagerness
17 Last trump
19 National
20 Enabled
22 Relieve
23 Tetrode
25 Iodide

64

Across
1 Kildare
5 Andante
9 Raked in the money
10 Away
11 Abhor
12 Anti
15 Look-see
16 Dudgeon
17 Miss out
19 All over
21 Naif
22 Brace
23 Snib
26 General practice
27 Dormant
28 Tenancy

Down
1 Kursaal
2 Like a dog's dinner
3 Andy
4 Ennoble
5 Ashford
6 Dump
7 Non-intervention
8 Elysian
13 Ascot
14 Oddly
17 Managed
18 Tartlet
19 Accurst
20 Robbery
24 Aria
25 Icon

65

Across
1 Gentleness
9 Seep
10 Industrial
11 Endear
12 Castile
15 Sceptic
16 Space
17 Neat
18 Lira
19 Act up
21 Endless
22 Romance
24 Theban
27 Drawbridge
28 Odds
29 Reflection

Down
2 Etna
3 Truest
4 Entails
5 Evil
6 Silence
7 Pedestrian
8 Appreciate
12 Convention
13 Stand ready
14 Epics
15 Scour
19 Asunder
20 Potable
23 Adrift
25 Calf
26 Agio

66

Across
1 Shake hands
6 Flip
10 Chair
11 Sauternes
12 Sentinel
13 Charm
15 Own goal
17 Dangles
19 Non-stop
21 Scourge
22 Piste
24 Anything
27 Osteopath
28 Utter
29 Flaw
30 Stinginess

Down
1 Sack
2 Agamemnon
3 Egret
4 Arsenal
5 Doubled
7 Linda
8 Pass muster
9 Bel canto
14 Soundproof
16 On the hop
18 Lorgnette
20 Play-act
21 Say when
23 Sutra
25 Houri
26 Iris

67

Across
1 Realism
5 Grapple
9 Firelight
10 Ankle
11 Enlarge
12 Auguste
13 Take stock
16 Slack
17 Solar
18 Comparing
21 Receipt
22 Narrate
25 Cacti
26 Animation
27 Sleighs
28 Nastier

Down
1 Reflect
2 April
3 Iller
4 Magneto
5 Get back
6 Analgesia
7 Pakistani
8 Ewe-neck
14 Kilocycle
15 Straining
17 Spruces
18 Cutlass
19 Mansion
20 Gleaner
23 Roams
24 Alibi

68

Across
1 Hides
4 Home Guard
8 Tempo
9 Go-between
11 Rats
12 Genie
13 Stay
16 Sleep like a top
19 Sweet nothings
20 Pump
22 Pique
23 Fair
26 Tête-à-tête
27 On ice
28 Rotterdam
29 Dined

Down
1 Hit-or-miss
2 Demitasse
3 Snow
4 High explosive
5 Goth
6 Alert
7 Dandy
10 British Museum
14 Recto
15 Jenny
17 Tasmanian
18 Pen friend
20 Peter
21 Motet
24 Lace
25 Bold

69

Across
1 Tacks
4 Exorcist
8 Encroach
9 Organist
11 Acclaim
13 Absentees
15 New Scotland Yard
18 Soporific
21 Hostage
22 Tameness
24 Casanova
25 Dark room
26 Eases

Down
1 The Marines
2 Cockcrow
3 Sporadic
4 Echo
5 Remain
6 Incite
7 Tart
10 Research
12 Mastiffs
14 Saddlebags
16 Dressage
17 Aviators
19 Pamper
20 Ranker
22 Tied
23 Scum

70

Across
1 Hard-headed
6 Emma
10 Recap
11 Terrorism
12 Convent
13 Dunster
14 Illustration
18 Self-catering
21 Exhumed
23 Pretext
24 Dominican
25 Input
26 Duct
27 Laryngitis

Down
1 Horace
2 Recent
3 Hip replacement
4 Antitrust
5 Erred
7 Maintain
8 Admiring
9 Mountaineering
15 Turn-penny
16 Ascended
17 Alchemic
19 Teapot
20 Otitis
22 Dicta

71

Across
7 Supporter
8 Attic
10 Perceive
11 Hoarse
12 Fell
13 Slogging
15 License
17 Fleecer
20 Sentence
22 Undo
25 Savant
26 Decadent
27 Pluck
28 Interests

Down
1 Muser
2 Apache
3 Articles
4 Reverse
5 Strangle
6 Dissenter
9 Theo
14 Liberally
16 Entrance
18 Launched
19 Leading
21 Note
23 Dodges
24 Anita

72

Across
1 Scream
5 Superman
9 Seconds out
10 Ahoy
11 Free will
12 Remote
13 Able
15 Flatmate
18 Footwear
19 Toss
21 Geyser
23 Holyhead
25 Wave
26 Hoity-toity
27 Aggrieve
28 Reduce

Down
2 Clear
3 Elopement
4 Madrid
5 Spoilt for choice
6 Peter Pan
7 Realm
8 Apostates
14 Boomerang
16 Matchwood
17 Search me
20 Player
22 Swear
24 Attic

73

Across
1 Gambler
5 Travail
9 Objective
10 Crown
11 Cortege
12 Tire out
13 Obligated
16 Ilion
17 Pence
18 Footnotes
21 Traitor
22 Lunette
25 Omega
26 Assertion
27 Estreat
28 Nostrum

Down
1 Groucho
2 Major
3 Lucre
4 Raiment
5 Treated
6 Accordion
7 Apologist
8 Long ton
14 Land-agent
15 Great Dane
17 Patmore
18 Far East
19 Only son
20 Sternum
23 Narks
24 Trier

74

Across
1 Stage right
9 Goya
10 Informally
11 Invest
12 Readier
15 Coterie
16 Roman
17 Cats
18 Dear
19 Serve
21 Buffalo
22 Exposed
24 To come
27 Peeping Tom
28 Opal
29 Red herring

Down
2 Tank
3 Ground
4 Rambler
5 Gill
6 Try it on
7 More or less
8 Cattle-grid
12 Rock bottom
13 Artificial
14 Romeo
15 Carve
19 Sleeper
20 Examine
23 Onager
25 Lead
26 Boon

75

Across
1 Hardship
6 Monica
9 Drawer
10 Thievery
11 Waterloo
12 Sultan
13 Fingerprints
16 Refreshments
19 Editor
21 A la carte
23 Sea-level
24 Divert
25 Steppe
26 Stealthy

Down
2 Adrian
3 Dowse
4 Hard lines
5 Pothole
6 Mails
7 Novelties
8 Currants
13 First slip
14 Panhandle
15 Dead heat
17 Measles
18 Starch
20 Revue
22 Anvil

76

Across

1 Handbarrow
6 Afar
9 Comet
10 Drivelled
12 Breathing-hole
14 Reaffirm
15 Mantis
17 Debunk
19 Moroccan
21 Go the distance
24 Lampshade
25 Id est
26 Yeti
27 Newsletter

Down

1 Hock
2 Namibia
3 Butterfingers
4 Redstart
5 Oribi
7 Fall out
8 Redressing
11 Egg mayonnaise
13 Prodigally
16 Fortress
18 Bath-mat
20 Clement
22 Image
23 Stir

77

Across

1 Repressed
9 Evasive
10 Abraham
11 In state
12 Protracts
14 At no time
15 Coarse
17 Present
20 Assure
23 Sack race
25 Oratorial
26 Aramaic
27 Necktie
28 Lorelei
29 Nectarine

Down

2 Embargo
3 Reactor
4 Seafarer
5 Desist
6 Passports
7 Titania
8 Reference
13 Tarsier
15 Constable
16 Sportable
18 Nastiest
19 Eclairs
21 Striker
22 Realign
24 Cochin

78

Across

1 Kitty
4 Discourse
9 Disturb
11 Abutter
12 Axis
13 Lodge
14 Bill
17 Paraphernalia
19 West Ham United
21 Scan
22 Hasty
23 Cave
26 Rapport
27 Hundred
28 Partridge
29 Wryly

Down

1 Kidnapped
2 Tastier
3 Your
5 Slanging match
6 Opus
7 Retsina
8 Enrol
10 Brokenhearted
15 Spasm
16 Bland
18 Wednesday
19 Wrapper
20 Tea tray
21 Scrap
24 Poor
25 Snow

79

Across

1 Charger
5 Guilder
9 Made out
10 Toppled
11 Airy-fairy
12 Tempe
13 Tense
15 In the dark
17 Hydrangea
19 Tacit
22 Gusto
23 Mannequin
25 Harvard
26 Apostle
27 Tessera
28 Destroy

Down

1 Compact
2 Andiron
3 Go off
4 Retailing
5 Get by
6 Impatient
7 Dilemma
8 Redneck
14 Elaborate
16 Trainband
17 High hat
18 Desires
20 Counter
21 Tannery
23 Media
24 Exons

80

Across

1 Baby-sitting
7 Needs
8 Agincourt
10 Eyeball
11 Debated
12 Lapse
13 Ancestral
16 Caretaker
18 Below
19 Antonym
22 Sherman
23 Treasurer
24 Tides
25 Swallowtail

Down

1 Bee-keeper
2 Bus-lane
3 Small-talk
4 Tried
5 Incubus
6 Grunt
7 Needlecraft
9 Tiddlywinks
14 Corkscrew
15 Role model
17 Tunisia
18 Beef tea
20 Tress
21 Moral

www.ingramcontent.com/pod-product-compliance
Ingram Content Group UK Ltd.
Pitfield, Milton Keynes, MK11 3LW, UK
UKHW040640280225
455688UK00002B/34